"From Rock

Roger ... ?????

Play away, please!!"

Ron Read

6/8/19

Starting the U.S. Open

From Shinnecock Hills to Pebble Beach

Ron Read

Fitting Words

Endorsements

- "When I came to the first tee and saw Ron, I said, 'Now it feels like the U.S. Open.'" ***Kirk Triplett***, Champions Tour player & veteran of eighteen U.S. Opens.

- "We shared a common goal—bringing our Open to the Northwest. He played a big part in finally making it happen at Chambers Bay." ***Peter Jacobsen***, 2004 U.S. Senior Open Champion.

- "Few have experienced the cauldron of every golfer's experiences on the first tee of the U.S. Open. My friend Ron Read had a front row seat, there, for twenty-three years, to witness the hardest shot in golf—the first one. He is in fact the man who was 'Starting the U.S. Open.'" ***Jim Nantz***, CBS Sports.

- "The first tee is not the same. Ron lent dignity that made you pay attention to the importance of the occasion. He also paid special attention to junior golfers in the gallery, too, making them feel a part of the Open." **Steve Frank**, fellow starter & 2018 President's Award recipient of the Southern California PGA.

- "It's fun for Ron to share his memories of friendships that he's made through golf over the years. Together, we smiled, laughed, and loved being a part of his 'up close-and-personal' stories and those about others we have admired. What a compliment it is that he included us down his 'Memory Lane' journey. We feel very special. Anyone who picks up this book will not be able to put it down." **Barbara & Jack Nicklaus**.

- "I couldn't sleep, thinking about walking with the best players in the world at Pebble Beach. That was followed by panic. . . . I still owe (Ron) one!" **Lyn Nelson**, former CEO, Northern California Golf Association.

- "It felt like a lion's den—playing with Retief in the final group. My heart was beating like a race horse. Then, I saw a friendly, familiar face—Ron's. He calmed my nerves." **Jason Gore**, golfer.

- "With the pressure of playing in our national championship, I was usually oblivious to my surroundings. It was always nice to see Ron's familiar face—cordial

- and professional." **Curtis Strange**, two-time U.S. Open champion.

- "Starting players was a helluva lot easier than taking their score-cards at the end of a tough day at the U.S. Open. I think he'd agree." **Curtis Strange**, 1988-89 U.S. Open Champion.

- "Was Ron nervous? Not as nervous as I was!" **Scott Williams,** among the first players I ever introduced, in 1986 at Shinnecock Hills.

- "My dad used warmth and wit in beautifully sharing the human side of the game, and he demonstrates that golf is still a game of character and integrity. This book is a legacy to his passion for golf, his career, and our family. We even learned so much through these stories." **Alicia Read Hoggan**.

- "Thank you for reminding me of some great memories and for taking my advice, 'Don't start anyone before the group's starting time.'" **Tom Meeks**, friend & USGA Championship Director.

- "Ron has been my friend for almost fifty years. He started me in my competitive years at our Open, and he started the groups I accompanied as a broadcaster. He did the job like FEDEX . . . on time and delivered." **Roger Maltbie**, NBC Golf.

- "Having officiated in the Rose Bowl, I knew big events. Seeing my old college roommate start golf's greatest—at Bethpage—was a big thrill for me, a nongolfer. This is a must-read for all." **Bob Holliday,** attorney and former Big 12 football umpire.

- "Ron is the only starter who pronounces every letter in a person's name. The first tee never sounded so good." **Steve Sands**, lead interviewer, NBC & Golf Channel.

- "Ron was the link in bringing the first U.S. Open to the Northwest at Chambers Bay. Like other great storytellers, he reports firsthand with the gift of insight and emotions for all—golfers and nongolfers, alike. Enjoy this read!" **Robert Trent Jones Jr.**, golf architect.

- "If you want to know what nervous *looks* like, ask Ron Read. He's seen it all." **Darrell Kestner,** eight-time, two-stage qualifier in U.S. Open and head professional at Deepdale Golf Club, Manhasset, New York.

- "Ron was golf's ultimate 'insider-insider.' In the over forty years he served golf, he worked with golf's greats—Jack, Arnie, Gary, Lee, Tom, Seve, Greg, and Tiger. Here, he gives you an insider's look at the U.S. Open and the USGA. This is a must for anyone who loves the game." **Tony Zirpoli**, friend and "Boss."

- "We worked together many times on the first tee, but it was on our long walks at Pebble Beach with his dog, Katrina, that I came to know he's a walking, talking Rolodex of golf characters. Many are in his book. It's a gem." **Dottie Pepper**, CBS Golf.

- "I always arrived at the first tee wanting my guy to win the U.S. Open. I still do. I bleed red, white, and blue." **Joe Lacava**, caddy for Tiger Woods and for 1992 Masters winner Fred Couples.

- "Ron was 'the man' on the first tee at the U.S. Open. He kindly welcomed you to the misery you were like to endure for the next few hours." **Brandel Chamblee**, Golf Channel commentator and author.

- "Ron did his best to pair a dad with his son—on Father's Day. He was overruled. By the way, Dad shot 71. His son, 81." **Jay Haas**, Bob Jones Award winner & Champions Tour golfer.

- "I lived Dad's stories. He had as much fun writing them as he did during his career serving this great game, all while seeing the goodness in others." **Ryan Read**.

- "Ron gave me an unexpected thrill on the first tee—a job as a referee." **Dick Clark**, attorney, Austin, Texas.

- "Ron was the E. F. Hutton of golf. When he spoke, people listened. He was the best at what he did and was one of golf's good guys." **Tom Lehman**, golfer.

- "Seeing Ron was comforting. He was the only starter to remind us to count our clubs." **Mike Carrick**, Tom Kite's caddy for twenty-one U.S. Opens.

- "When I heard, 'Ladies & gentlemen, this is the 7:30 starting time. From Coral Springs, Florida . . . **Steve Scott**. "my heart pounded even harder."

Published by Fitting Words LLC
www.fittingwords.net

Cover design by 360 Media Group
Cover photo courtesy of Joanne Dost, authorized photographer of Pebble Beach Company

Pebble Beach, Pebble Beach Golf Links, Pebble Beach Resorts and The Lone Cypress, their related marks and images, are all trademarks and trade dress owned by Pebble Beach Company. Used with permission.

ISBN: 978-1-7322391-5-9

Printed in the United States of America
1 2 3 4 5 6 7 — 25 24 23 22 21 20 19

To my wife, Missy, my loving family, and so many friends made through the wonderful game of golf. This book is also in honor of my parents, Edna and Ike, who introduced me to this great game and to my childhood neighbor, Albie, who provided me a field of dreams.

Contents

Acknowledgments

U NENDING GRATITUDE IS EXPRESSED TO SO MANY WHO ENCOURAGED, COUNSELED, and contributed to this book. To those I may have missed, you're in my heart. Trust me. Dan Wright, Mike Towle, Melissa Miller, J. P. Marks, Jess Hershey, Melissa Wilson, George Peper, Tony Zirpoli, Larry Adamson, Peter Crabtree, Jim Nantz, Barbara & Jack Nicklaus, Tom Lehman, Steve Sands, Steve Scott, Rich Skyzinski, Alicia Read Hoggan, Missy Read, Katrina Read, William Read, Jim White, Jim Jenkins, Ryan Read, Curtis Strange, Jason Gore, Dottie Pepper, Robert Trent Jones Jr., Trent Jones, Dr. Mark Mammel, Steve Frank, Peter Jacobsen, Jay Haas, Brandel Chamblee, Hema Hattangady, Joe Lacava, Tom Meeks, Ed Sease, Scott Williams, Darrell Kestner, Andy Dillard, Lyn Nelson, Kirk Triplett, Jaime Diaz, John Feinstein, Don Dormer, Missy Jones, Charles Winton, Dr. Tom Loss, Dr. Howdy Giles, Tim Moraghan, Bob Holliday, Roger Maltbie, Marty Parkes, Jack Holt, Sam Trust, Nick LaRocca, Professor Robert Puelz, Robert "Bo" Links, Mike Viron, Jacques de Spoelberch, Roger Harvie, Jim Farrell, Don Wilson, Gene Westmoreland, Dave Buckingham, John "Bud" Johnson. Jerry Tarde, Don Wilson, Donn Wilkerson, Mark Loomis, Denis Peavy, Alex Hulanicki, and Steve Foehl.

Introduction: My Journey

THIS IS NOT MY FAVORITE PART OF THE BOOK. IT IS ABOUT ME. I am more comfortable telling stories about the goodness of others. That comes later.

Besides, it is not easy to explain how a boy, once kidnapped and from an unprivileged background, found his way to the first tee of the U.S. Open as its starter.

It's been an amazing journey.

My childhood was fun, though not perfect. Some might say it was dysfunctional and, in some ways, yes, I might ask for a mulligan.

I was the only child of Edna Conrad Anderson. In 1943, at age eighteen, she married Charles Thomas Anderson, twenty-five, who was serving in the Army Air Corps during World War II. I was born Ronald Reece Anderson on October 6, 1944.

Their marriage did not last. To this day, I don't know why it dissolved. Their ages (more hers) and their financial struggles probably played a part. They divorced in 1947.

"Chuck" Anderson was not permitted to see me often. During a rare visitation on a Friday afternoon in 1947, he kidnapped me, technically speaking. Without legal authority, he flew me to live in a beach community south of Los Angeles. After a short time, he realized he could not cope with the unhappiness of a young son separated from his mother. He and I returned to Chicago's Municipal Airport, now called Midway. All I remember was a very bumpy flight to Chicago. Appropriately, the turbulence prepared him for the reception he received. Mom and my grandfather retrieved me. This was the last time I recall ever seeing him.

My dear aunt, Mary Lou, has shared much about the distant past.

Mom was one of eight siblings. She was the fifth child born to Florence and Albert Conrad, who had five sons and three daughters. Florence died on the birth of their last child, Neal.

Before you leap to a conclusion about the sadness of my childhood, it was not unhappy. I was surrounded by a closely knit family. It was like having eight brothers and sisters.

I called my grandfather "Pawp." He was the head of a very loving family. His eight children cared for each other in tough financial times.

"We don't have much money," my aunts and uncles often said, "but we sure eat well."

The Conrads lived in a remote area out in the country, south of LaGrange and west of Chicago. Pawp's home was farmlike and modest. Its doors were never locked. There was a barn, but no animals. The house was located on old Route 66, once the busiest highway in America. This explains my aversion to noisy traffic.

Pawp became my surrogate father. He reared the nine of us—by himself. He taught his family to be as honest as Abe Lincoln. It was easy for him. He lived it. His example served each of us well throughout our lives.

His children attended Lyons Township High School but none of them went on to college after high school. Instead, the men served our country—either in the army or navy. All eight married. Mom was the only one to ever divorce.

Pawp and little Ronny (me) were inseparable. He was the rock of my early life.

It is amazing how Pawp provided for his family by pushing a broom, literally. He swept floors at the Electro-Motive plant, where train engines were made. The E-M plant was said to be the largest manufacturing facility in the U.S.

Pawp had at least one side job. He mowed a church cemetery. Needing help, and perhaps companionship, he took his buddy—me, age five—with him to the cemetery. It was my first job. Nineteen other jobs followed that one in my youth. He taught me how to push a lawnmower, respectfully, around tombstones.

Several relatives were at rest in that cemetery. Mom and my stepfather, Ike, now rest there.

After a day of work at the cemetery, we spent evenings listening to our beloved

Chicago White Sox on radio. I can still hear Bob Elson calling Minnie Minoso's home run a "White Owl Wallop" over the 362-foot wall at Comiskey Park.

My favorite player was second baseman Nellie Fox. He didn't hit many home runs, but he didn't strike out, either. Nellie wore No. 2 on his uniform, but he was No. 1 in our hearts.

My adulation of Nellie Fox helps say something about me.

Nellie was finally inducted into baseball's Hall of Fame in 1997—twenty-two years after his death. I flew from Maui to L.A. and on to Chicago, then to Newark to attend the induction ceremony. I rented a car and drove to Albany, New York. The next morning was a dream, my only trip to the Baseball Hall of Fame in Cooperstown. At the inductions, Mrs. Fox stole the show on a day when popular Dodger manager Tommy Lasorda was also honored.

Pawp left us in May 1975, five months before Nellie died. Pawp's cheer was heard at Nellie's induction. He was happy I made the effort to be there.

The depth of feeling for family, friends, and acquaintances for those who touched my life has always been strong.

The same feelings drew me to attend memorials for Payne Stewart and Arnold Palmer. I would not have missed those occasions, either.

When I wasn't attempting to play baseball like Nellie Fox while growing up, I was learning how to hit down on a golf ball to make it go up. My clubs were hand-me-down Kroydons, left-handed, like my batting style.

Pawp's yard wasn't long enough for me to hit full shots. So I begged help from our next-door neighbor, Albie Hollands.

"Albie, may I mow your field so that I can hit balls?" I'd ask. How could he refuse?

My experience in mowing the cemetery had paid off. The result was my own shaggy field of dreams.

There was a bowling alley across Albie's field on Route 66. It also had a lighted driving range. While Mom worked days as a waitress, l dodged trucks to cross the busy highway. The driving range manager was a tough ex-Marine with a crew cut. When he wasn't looking, I would sneak out to hunt and find balls in the rough. They were the aged, striped balls that could not be retrieved with a ball-picker on the back of his Jeep. With pockets filled, I ran back across the road, hoping he did not see me.

Pawp knew I was racing between trucks across that highway, but he never squealed to Mom.

"Ronny, look both ways," he admonished.

When Pawp and I were not watching the White Sox or Ed Sullivan on our black-and-white TV, we occasionally watched *All Star Golf*. Colorful pro Jimmy Demaret commentated on matches with pros such as Sam Snead, Porky Oliver, and Arnold Palmer. They became my golf instructors into my teens.

Baseball and basketball remained my favorite games. My goal was always the same, to be a left-handed Nellie Fox, my idol.

* * *

When I entered kindergarten at Ideal School, Mom had met another man—Wilbur Gordon Read. He was known as "Ike" by countless friends, and he married Mom in 1952.

It was a simple time. Americans had elected Dwight Eisenhower as president. The decorated general was known simply as Ike. I was eight years old at the time. Kids, who knew nothing about politics, chanted on the playground—"I like Ike!"—echoing what we heard at home.

On a personal level, I did like Ike, my stepdad. He adopted me when I was nine. I became Ronald Reece Read—yes, RRR.

President Ike and my new father, Ike, both loved golf. They stimulated my interest in the game, but golf was game No. 3 for me.

After Mom and Ike were married, the new Read Family lived with Pawp on Route 66. Dad started a printing business in the house's barn.

We had few neighbors. My playmates were all girls—Judy Holland, daughter of Albie, and sisters Joanie and Patsie Belasich. Another girl—Janet Lynch—was in Mrs. Good's third-grade class.

Janet's dad was my first baseball instructor and someone who impacted my life.

Sherrill Lynch coached the LaGrange Highlands Little League's Electro-Motive Cubs. In preparation for the 1953 season, he held a pre-season program, indoors, at Ideal School in the heart of Chicago's chilling winter. Because of the third-grade connection to his daughter, he invited me, age eight, to his evening program.

Mr. Lynch taught kids baseball—its rules, batting, bunting, throwing, and fielding ground balls on the hardwood gym floor at Ideal School. Then, in a classroom setting, he taught life lessons.

"Winners never quit, and quitters never win," he instilled.

Mr. Lynch demanded acts of sportsmanship, such as picking up the catcher's mask and wiping it clean of dirt before handing it to the catcher. And, after the game, win or lose, we were instructed to remove our caps, look our opponents in the eye, and shake their hands—while offering congratulations. Six decades later, I have never forgotten that.

During those pre-season drills, Mr. Lynch saw potential in my ability, and he wanted me to be a Cub. There was one problem. Having had a perfect 18-0 record in 1952, he would select last. He speculated another team might pick me, but the cunning manager had a plan. He met privately with Mom.

"Tell Ronny not to try," Mr. Lynch told Edna Read.

Mr. Lynch wanted me to "sandbag" my ability.

To Mom, those were fighting words. Of German descent, she was not shy of opinion, and she had a religious sense of right and wrong. Mr. Lynch's request was sinful. Mom never swore, but I am certain her response was colorful. It meant "no."

A few months after that chat, Edna's son ran onto his first baseball field near Electro-Motive's gigantic plant. It was a cold and damp spring day, and 128 kids attended the tryouts.

I gave 110 percent. When tested with fly balls to outfielders, I circled, trying to find the ball in the gray sky. It was not like the ceiling at Ideal School. Every ball fell to the ground. Luckily, I avoided being bonked on the head.

It got no better when ground balls were hit to us on the stony infield. Most balls went through my legs. They didn't have the perfect bounce off the school's hardwood floor.

Kids around me laughed.

Because of my dismal performance, nobody picked me. I was the last one left among all those kids. Mr. Lynch got his wish. By default, I became a Cub.

Months later, the Cubs were again champs, 18-0 for the season.

Teammates Bobby Burdett, Harry Bohn and Billy Krohn, all twelve, made the all-star team.

After batting 0-for-the-first-half of the season, I had a better second half. I was selected an alternate to the all-star team. Mr. Lynch smiled. I had Nellie Fox's job in sight.

Twenty years later, Mom shared with me the appeal Mr. Lynch had made to her prior to my 1953 tryout experience. I never knew. She was still mad at Mr. Lynch, but we laughed.

The man was human. Besides, Mr. Lynch had gifted us something more important—play fairly, respect others, and give it your all.

My feelings for baseball remained strong. For four years, I played first base at Lyons Township High School. Teammates voted me MVP of our championship team my sophomore year. That MVP recognition would be traded, today, gladly, for a win over Decatur Eisenhower in the final game of the Illinois State Championship my senior year. Learning to lose was a tough, but valuable, lifelong lesson.

* * *

High school basketball had become a passion for me. Coach Sandusky kept me on the varsity team, I am certain, only to condition me for baseball. Warming the bench, supporting teammates, was also a good lesson.

I also learned the world did not revolve around me. Long walks home after winter basketball practices underscored that, too. I walked a lot. Little was ever handed to me. Neither were car keys.

My baseball pals and I dabbled at golf on Chicago's excellent public courses. I was never competitive. Golf was never more than a game—a wonderful pastime with friends.

After Dad's printing business grew, he moved it from Pawp's barn to nearby Brookfield.

Mom and Dad worked long hours in their business. After they experienced modest success, they joined a nine-hole club on the outskirts of Chicago. They were keen golfers. Mom was very athletic in her youth, and she could have been an excellent golfer. We just had fun.

Nothing, yet, indicated I might make a career serving golf someday or become starter at the U.S. Open.

Academically, I was a conscientious student—a good one, though a three-iron from valedictorian. LTHS was an excellent, competitive public high school of thirty-four hundred students.

* * *

Baseball presented me with an opportunity to play at Western Michigan University. Instead, I elected to study accounting at Drake University. Goals changed after my freshman year of college. Advertising became my focus, with a minor in psychology. The dream of becoming a Nellie Fox successor was forgotten.

The early 1960s were pivotal for all of us. The Cuban Missile Crisis and the threat of a nuclear war introduced reality to fun-loving college students.

During this time, I worked evenings at Wakonda Club, host of the 1963 U.S. Amateur. It allowed me to see national championship golf "up close." That experience had a significant impact, though I did not realize it at the time.

Months later, in November 1963, the world was paralyzed for days following the assassination of President Kennedy. We all remember the exact time and place we learned of the tragedy.

Then came the Vietnam War. During these tumultuous times, I was an ROTC candidate, expecting to become an Air Force officer after graduation. Plans changed in the summer of 1964. My family doctor confirmed I had a heart murmur. He opined that the condition would make me ineligible for the military, as everyone in the Conrad family had faithfully done. Because of my heart condition, there was little reason to complete the ROTC program. I dropped out of the four-year program.

After graduating from Drake in 1966, I received a draft notice ordering me to report for a physical at 5:30 A.M. "PROMPTLY" in Berwyn, Illinois, where it turns out I had been born. My doctor's diagnosis and assessment of my military fitness proved wrong. I passed the physical!

As the old saying goes, "You're in the army now!"

In June 1967, I reported to the army to begin my two-year commitment. After I completed basic training at Fort Leonard Wood, Missouri, the army ordered me to the Defense Department's language school in Monterey, California. I wouldn't trade that duty or the army experience. It, too, was life changing.

My first day in Monterey was September 8, 1967—the same day I met my future wife, Missy. We married in June 1969. During our courtship, she made something clear: she was not leaving California. We shared two loves—each other and the Monterey Peninsula. We stayed on the Peninsula, and I began a job search.

My focus turned to golf, not as a player, but in serving the game. Seeds that had been planted inside of me at the 1963 U.S. Amateur were embedded and growing. I reached out to the Northern California Golf Association, which had facilitated the building of Spyglass Hill Golf Course in Pebble Beach. With its offices above the ninth green, I envisioned that setting better than Madison Avenue, where a successful advertising executive might someday find himself.

Twenty NCGA board members interviewed me at Diablo Country Club. They grilled me for an hour before finally allowing me to ask one question. I was petrified.

"Will you please hire me?" It was all I could muster.

They gave me the job—actually, a career. Serving the game became my passion. For forty-three years, I gave golf the same effort of that baseball tryout in 1953, always remembering, "Winners never quit, and quitters never win."

* * *

Good fortune again came my way.

I was an understudy to Bob Hanna, the organization's executive director. Bob was, to me, the Joe Dey of regional amateur golf.

Mr. Dey was the USGA's head for thirty-four years, then he became the PGA Tour's first commissioner. Bob and Mr. Dey were friends and they were from the same mold—traditionalists. Bob learned golf at Oak Hill Country Club in Rochester, New York, where he caddied for Walter Hagen. He graduated from Cal-Berkeley, competing on the Bears golf team. Like Mr. Dey, Bob's accomplishments in serving golf warrant his selection in any golf hall of fame.

Working with Bob, I learned from the ground up. Together, we pioneered many services. We were the first advocates for the USGA's national Golf Handicap and Information Network (GHIN) system. The Obstacle Course Rating System (OCRS) was created under our auspices. OCRS was later adopted by the USGA. We were not the inventors of the Slope System. Dr. Clyne Soley and Trygve Bogevold were, but we tested the new system for them at NCGA clubs.

Bob and I facilitated the creation of a ladies association in Northern California for those women who played nine holes by their choice.

We also started a program to train club personnel in emergency resuscitation from heart attacks.

We initiated a membership program for golfers who traveled, rather than identifying themselves as members of only one facility. The program resulted in the NCGA's becoming the country's largest association of amateur golfers.

Later, we conceived Poppy Hills Golf Club, thus becoming the first amateur association to own and operate its own golf course. A front-row seat gave me a broad understanding of so much in golf. I had learned from a true golf icon, Bob Hanna.

* * *

In July 1981, John Laupheimer asked me to become the USGA's manager of Western Regional Affairs. Ten minutes after I accepted the offer, John called back to tell me he had just resigned to become LPGA commissioner. I was his last official act.

The USGA gave me a big assignment. My principal role was to strengthen relations with associations in ten states, from Alaska and Hawaii, to Montana and New Mexico. Later, Texas was added. I was a frequent traveler.

None of this was possible without support from home in Pebble Beach. Missy was the pillar—like Pawp—in rearing two wonderful children. Alicia graduated from Miami University in Ohio and is a mother of two. Ryan graduated from Washington & Lee University and is co-founder of healthy Day One Treats for dogs.

During my journey, I wondered if I were possibly the first person to pursue a career serving golf after schooling.

Friends like Tom Meeks, Tony Zirpoli, David Fay, Jay Mottola, Steve Foehl, Tom Morgan, and Denny Davenport gravitated to serving golf, but only after pursuing other careers. If I was first, I needed the early start on these very talented friends.

There was still no sign that I would become the first-tee starter at the U.S. Open.

Starting the U.S. Open

1

Starting — My Style

I T WAS A JOB I NEVER SOUGHT NOR ONE THAT COULD EVER BE CALLED WORK. In 1986, I found myself drafted for a second time in my life. The first was the U.S. Army. This time, it was to become the starter of the U.S. Open. Both proved to be great honors.

No preparation came with the assignment, and there was very little instruction.

Everything else evolved over the next twenty-four years—what to do, what to say, and even what to wear. I was left to create what I thought appropriate for our National Championship of American golf. It was flattering, later, to see the same protocol used at U.S. Opens and other events after my departure.

P. J. Boatwright Jr., who directed the USGA's s Rules and Competitions Department and oversaw the conduct of the U.S. Open, offered three instructions before sending me to the first tee in 1986:

1. Keep it simple. 2. Say the player's name and hometown. 3. Stay on time.

That was it. Period.

But I learned it wasn't that simple.

Before grabbing the bullhorn at Shinnecock Hills, a story was shared about another starter.

The incident occurred at the U.S. Women's Open, where Mrs. Kelly, a USGA volunteer, was a starter for the first time. She asked P. J. what to say.

Lore had it P. J. gave the same instructions he gave me.

"But how do I send them off?" she asked.

"Just say," P. J. offered, "'Let it rip!'"

Mrs. Kelly followed instructions perfectly—names and hometowns. Then she ended with, "Let it rip!"

If true, here's hoping the player was JoAnne Carner. She'd laugh at such a moment.

Well, P. J. didn't laugh. He was in the drive zone on the first hole. When he heard Mrs. Kelly, he made a quick U-turn and returned to the first tee. This time, he suggested a different approach.

"Why don't you say, 'Play away, please?'" he said.

P. J. borrowed those words from The Old Course at St. Andrews, where the starter instructs golfers, "Play away."

I adopted that sendoff. It just seemed right. Others who approached me often thought so, too. The goal was to create a decorum that was appropriate for the U.S. Open and respectful to the game.

Before the introduction of players, there was much to do in preparation. We had a checklist of items on the first tee. It included scorecards, pencils, a "Notice to Competitors" with local rules, rule books, matches for the smokers, tees, and hole-location sheets.

In the early days, a bullhorn was used. Everything was in place an hour before play.

I didn't need a clock. My $39 watch was accurate to the second.

Players normally arrived three or four minutes before their start. A few dallied, like Davis Love III and Vijay Singh. They didn't leave much time for instructions.

In those few minutes, players met others and took care of business. Some had never met their fellow competitors, like those from pro tours around the world. Others were the qualifiers, numbering about fifty in the field of 156. Most of those were not familiar names.

After players met, they were introduced to usually eager volunteers—a referee, a walking scorer, and a standard bearer who carried a scoreboard. Gathering players and volunteers together was not an easy task. It was like corralling horses without a lasso.

Volunteers were always wide-eyed in meeting the players.

Then the business began. Players received instructions, along with a stack of papers. Most of those went unread and were immediately stuffed somewhere in their golf bags.

The most important document they received was a scorecard. Player A received player B's card; B kept C's; and C received A's. There was a reason for this system. Occasionally, the scoring volunteer needed to double check a score. The system aided the scorer in knowing who had whose scorecard. Generally, the less conversation with players, the better. The system helped.

Lee Trevino was the exception. His chatter was well-documented.

Players and caddies wanted one thing—the hole-location sheet. To them, nothing else mattered. They gobbled them in large numbers, and my supply had to be replenished frequently over nine hours on the first tee. They immediately began to focus on the location of every hole.

Nobody focused more than Phil Mickelson. Playing in his first U.S. Open in 1990 at Medinah, Phil's approach as a nineteen-year-old amateur was revealing. Every day, he studied the hole location on No. 1, then hit four different shots with several different clubs over the four rounds. He tied for 29th, and I thought, "This guy's going to be good."

My attempt to interest the players in reading another important bit of information—the "Notice to Competitors"—was a losing and hopeless proposition. Perhaps one in ten scanned the lengthy document. I did not blame them. The Notice listed the temporary immovable obstructions (TIOs) they might encounter during the round. That is a long term for the intrusions to playing golf. TIOs are things erected for the championship—such as grandstands, concessions, and hospitality chalets. When players encounter TIOs, they call for officials. Players know they are better off relying on the assistance of a well-qualified referee rather than run the risk of misinterpreting the complex TIO rule, then dropping in a wrong place. Why take a chance?

Next, players were asked to identify their golf balls to fellow competitors. If necessary, it was suggested they use an indelible marking pen. They took this act seriously.

It helped prevent a violation for playing a wrong ball, a preventable occurrence. Sadly, it still happens in deep U.S. Open rough.

"If you haven't played a wrong ball, you will," Tom Meeks liked to say. Meeks was second in command in the Rules and Competitions Department when I started at the USGA and took over after P. J. Boatwright passed away in 1991.

Duffy Waldorf was known for marking his ball. The evening before every round, he painted balls for the next day. They became art pieces. He once gave me a ball just before a TV starting time. It said, "Just Smile." Duffy must have suffered Meeks's prediction in his past.

My last advice to players was a friendly reminder. "Please count your clubs."

The reminder occasionally saved a player from violating the fourteen-club rule. It sometimes served as a reminder that he might be carrying a club he did not want that day and had forgotten to take it out.

"Gentlemen, good luck!" Those were final words I'd say before the start of introductions.

It was time to play golf.

In my twenty-three years on the first tee, everyone started on time.

Well, we paused a couple times. The first was at the start of the 1990 U.S. Open at Medinah. After introducing Britt Tuttle, player No. 1, of Orlando, a procession of ducks began a march directly toward the first tee. They did so every day at 7 A.M. We worked around Mother Nature.

Nobody minded the interruption. It was nice that the quacks broke the silence and the tension.

2

The Little Watch That Could

NOWADAYS, CLOCKS ARE PROMINENTLY PLACED ON THE FIRST TEE AT MOST MAJOR and professional tournaments. Some events even designate them as the "official" time, and they position the big clocks on every tee. While they might be official, I learned they do not always keep exact time.

At Pinehurst in 2005, a large clock debuted behind me on the first tee. It was positioned to get plenty of TV exposure. The big clock had one problem: It was not accurate. It was one minute off. That's not good enough in golf.

At Oakmont, two years later, the big clock was back. It was reasonably accurate to the minute, but it had no second hand. It still does not.

In 2006, the big clock was not alone. Another clock was bestowed as a back-up. This clock was atomic, and it provided accurate digital time—when it worked.

At the U.S. Open of 2007, Western Pennsylvania's temperatures approached 100 degrees, and when the sun hit the atomic clock, the clock quit—went black. Its time was invisible.

Thankfully, I still wore my $39 wristwatch. It kept perfect time to the second for more than twenty years and was my "official" timepiece of the U.S. Open. Its brand will remain my secret. It's second to none.

Technology might be great—when it works.

3

Life at the First Tee:
Welcome to Show Biz

M Y VOICE WAS NOT SOOTHING, LIKE RADIO'S EARL NIGHTINGALE OR TV'S JIM NANTZ. Nor was it bold, like actor James Earl Jones. I was not comfortable hearing mine. Thus, I never willfully watched television replays from the first tee.

However, I was caught off guard one day while watching NBC from my couch at home a year after leaving the first tee. There was my voice doing the introduction of Tiger Woods. It was used in U.S. Open promotional spots. Again, hearing my voice frightened me.

NBC's surprise brought back the memory of Frank Hannigan's final words when he sent me to the first tee for the final round in 1986:

"Welcome to show biz," Frank said.

My goal on the first tee was to create a decorum appropriate for the world's most important championship. For the players, this was their place of business. It was also where many began the pursuit of their boyhood dreams—those of winning the U.S. Open.

Creating the right atmosphere was often easier planned than accomplished. In 1993 at Baltusrol, for example, it was chaotic, leaving me slightly embarrassed.

Traditionally, the starters in practice rounds were officials from the state golf association or local PGA section. They shared this prestigious duty. At Baltusrol, two celebrities were added. They were famous basketball coaches and TV analysts—Bill Raftery of CBS and P. J. Carlesimo. I learned they were also comedians.

They entertained players and fans and, frankly, they were hilarious.

Their entertainment skills became clear on Wednesday, the day before the first round.

Dr. Howdy Giles and I visited the first tee. I was on a scouting mission, getting a lay of the land. Howdy was about to be interviewed by ESPN. He was a top rules official who happened to be Arnold Palmer's longtime friend and dentist. What we witnessed was raucous, not the business-like atmosphere we expected. The starters were having fun! So were the players and fans. It felt more like a friendly Monday pro-am. It was definitely not a typical U.S. Open scene. I realized Thursday morning's start would be a challenge. Things had to change—and fast.

I was right.

Thursday was like no other opening round. Players wandered on the first tee. Caddies stood everywhere. Scoring volunteers were not on time to meet the players. Standard bearers needed instructions. TV cameramen left their roped media area to roam anywhere they pleased. More people were inside the ropes than outside. At times, I could not see the players through the crowd of folks in front of me. This starter was clearly not in charge. The melee led to a memorable, though embarrassing, moment.

Five hours into play, we still didn't have proper order. At 12:20, the players were Jay Don Blake, John Huston, and Jim Thorpe. Then another VIP showed up. It was USGA president Stu Bloch. He surprised me by his visit. Actually, this was his second visit. Earlier, he had come and suffered a misfortune. A bird hit his new U.S. Open cap. This time, he had a new cap, and I surmised he was there checking to see how I was performing. I tried to be on my best behavior but failed badly. What Stu witnessed left him wondering.

I introduced Jay Don Blake. That went perfectly, but his drive was not. He pulled the ball left, badly, probably out of bounds. Next, John Huston drove safely into the fairway. Third to play was Jim Thorpe. What happened next challenged Jim's affable nature.

I already knew that someone was going to play a second ball—a provisional—because of the errant drive, but then I blanked.

Jim teed his ball and prepared to swing. As I watched, something didn't seem right to me as he drew the club back.

"Jim, is this a provisional ball?" I interrupted.

My intention was honorable. I had not heard him say the words required by the rules, "This a provisional ball."

This rocked Jim. He managed to stop his swing. He looked back at me and proclaimed, "Man, I haven't even hit a ball yet and you guys (USGA) are trying to penalize me!"

President Bloch mumbled, "What just happened here?"

Only then did I realize I had not yet introduced Jim. It was Jay Don Blake who required a provisional ball, not Jim. I attempted a fast recovery.

"And from Buffalo, New York . . . Jim Thorpe. Play away, please."

It was a triple bogey—mine.

The good news was that Jim quickly composed. His long drive came to rest in the center of the fairway.

I'd known Jim for twenty years and knew his family story. He was the ninth of twelve children. That might have conditioned him to confusion, but nothing was like this, all of it my creation.

I raced to apologize. He is a big man, a former running back at Morgan State. I attempted to give him a hug. My arms could not reach around him. There was no time for an explanation. We just laughed. President Bloch did not. He looked like a guy who'd locked his keys in his courtesy car.

After Thursday's tumultuous start, nothing would be left to chance. I painted Xs on the ground. Friday's instructions were, "Caddies, stand here. Scorers, please stand over there."

During my remaining years on the first tee, I vowed there would never be another moment like that with poor Jim Thorpe.

As U.S. Open player liaison in the years before I became a starter, I traveled to PGA Tour events to listen to players' gripes, suggestions, and concerns. Some had strong feelings. Issues varied.

A recurring theme was that our officials were overly officious. Others opined about our attire. They said our Rules Committee officials looked silly, even pompous, wearing dark blue jackets and ties on June's hot, humid days.

Lee Trevino quipped, "When I reach sixty, I'm gonna buy a blue blazer and a can of dandruff and run the USGA." If anyone could cut to the chase, it was Trevino. The rigid attire had to go.

Peter Jacobsen put it another way. "We can't relate to Rules guys in coats and ties on hot summer days." This came from a very reasoned guy.

I took those views to USGA's Golf House headquarters in New Jersey. For four years, I tried, unsuccessfully, to change the culture and to relax the attire of officials. Change finally came in 1986.

It took a casual guy, C. Grant Spaeth, chairman of the Championship, to finally relax the dress code for officials. He instructed all USGA staff and officials to show up in white golf shirts and khaki pants. No ties! That would be the attire for the week. The new look applied on the first tee, too.

Did the relaxed appearance improve player relations? Nope. Grousing continued.

A few years later, Jacobsen surprised me with a change of heart. "We like you better the old way." Peter realized that a level of respect came from the more formal look, even on the golf course. That was his good upbringing. I attribute that to his dad, Erling, who instilled a deep respect for the game in Peter and his brother, David.

The more casual look continued for most officials, but not necessarily me. In 1992 at Pebble Beach, ABC dictated my attire. The network demanded a blazer and tie, feeling that one should dress properly "when you are star of stage and screen." Their words, not mine. Blazer and tie worked OK in the coolness of the Monterey Peninsula, but not Pittsburgh's Oakmont or New York's Winged Foot.

Later, I was given some discretion.

In 1999 at Pinehurst, I added a traditional look. I wore a bow tie. When Vijay Singh came to the first tee, he greeted me, "Did you lose a bet?" The bow tie remained through 2010. The jacket was off in oppressive heat, when I rebelled.

I used to wear the ever-stylish bucket hat, but in 1991, Spaeth, then the president of the USGA, gave me another order, "Read, get rid of the bucket hat." Grant won that match, too.

* * *

Players had their own individual pre-start routines. Their habits became predictable.

After players arrived, I introduced one to another, though in many groups, most knew each other from the various tours. But at the U.S. Open, there were new faces—the qualifiers, to include a number of amateurs. After formally meeting, players met the rules officials, volunteer scorers, and standard bearers who would accompany them.

Next came instructions to players and distribution of hole-location sheets, introduced in the early eighties. Until then, most caddies walked the course, pre-dawn, to get yardages and hole positions that were otherwise unavailable pre-round. With the advent of hole-location sheets, most caddies stopped the morning march. That pleased the hundreds who prepared the course—mowing, raking, setting tees, and cutting holes. They didn't like having 156 caddies getting in the way. Complex yardage booklets and hole sheets didn't deter one caddie—Fanny Sunesson, who never stopped her morning course inspections. She worked for Nick Faldo and then Henrik Stenson, and that woman was good.

Generally, chitchat was minimal on the first tee. I left players alone. We seldom carried on casual conversations. Occasionally, they had rules questions, but most went into their personal "cocoons," looked at the day's hole locations, or talked with their caddies.

A few often wanted to talk. Fred Couples usually had several questions ready for me. Fred fired away as though he'd been thinking about things for days. We always had a very good relationship. However, once, at Pinehurst in 2005, I had to speak with him like a father-to-a-naughty-son. This was after he had made an inappropriate comment to a spectator in the gallery. Still, I relish our relationship.

Conversation on the first tee was light and varied. On Sunday, usually Father's Day at the U.S. Open, I extended good wishes to those I knew to be dads, and we talked about kids. It seemed to relax them, thinking about their dads and being fathers, rather than the U.S. Open at hand.

Occasionally, we killed a minute or two chatting. Sixty seconds before his start at Bethpage in 2002, Thomas Bjorn initiated a brief discussion.

The upcoming Ryder Cup at The Belfry in England a few months away was already on his mind. He asked if I would be there. The untimeliness of his question caught me off guard. Thomas was surprised at my response.

"No, the Ryder Cup has gotten too commercial," I said. "You (pros) have made it about money. I prefer the low-key nature of the Walker Cup. Money does not matter."

"I agree," he responded. "We play for too much money."

Ten seconds later, I looked at my $39 watch. It was time to start.

"Please welcome from Silkeborg, Denmark . . . Thomas Bjorn." Sixteen years later, Bjorn's passion was fulfilled. He was captain of a winning European Ryder Cup team.

* * *

Over time, I learned Lucas Glover and David Duval were voracious readers. I could count on them to share the name of a good book.

Least talkative?

It was Tiger Woods. We never spoke. He was laser-focused, like no other. I attempted to engage him in conversation once—in 2004. I had been around Tiger many times over a decade and a half, though we'd never really spoken. When he arrived on the first tee, I thought, "There's always a first time."

"What do you think of your new golf coach at Stanford?" I asked. Stanford icon Bob Murphy had told me it was going to be Casey Martin, a college teammate of Woods's at Stanford. I thought this "news" would please Tiger. I was wrong.

"It's not Casey," he growled. "It's Conrad Ray."

Tiger was right. We never spoke again. We were last together on a courtesy bus at Chambers Bay. Joe Lacava, now Tiger's caddie, and I carried on a pleasant conversation. Tiger was across the way, about six feet away—focused. He always was.

It was now time for their last instruction.

"Gentlemen, please count your clubs." That reminder became a tradition as one of the last things I'd say to players before they started a round.

Every group received this instruction every day, ever since Oak Hill in 1989. Its genesis was, again, Grant Spaeth.

"Do you ask the players to count their clubs?" the Championship Chairman asked.

"Grant, this is the big leagues," I said. "No, I don't."

"If one player goes off the tee with too many clubs," Grant advised with a smile, "you'll be in the little leagues."

I got the message. From that moment until my final appearance in 2010, every player was asked. Some probably tired hearing it. A few became proactive. The first thing they said upon walking onto the first tee was, "We've counted our clubs."

My intention was to protect players from a rules violation. It was a reminder to those who might have added or changed clubs overnight.

I have often been asked, "Would the violation Ian Woosnam received in 2001 for too many clubs in the Open Championship happen at the U.S. Open?" No, it would not happen while I was on the first tee, and it never did. Well, once. More on that later.

The reminder saved several players. One claimed a national championship because of it.

At the 1999 U.S. Senior Open at Des Moines Golf & Country Club in Iowa, Dave Eichelberger's caddie, Bobby Conlan, arrived on the first tee and, said, "We've already counted our clubs."

Two minutes later, Eichelberger came to me carrying a putter—one that was not his. He'd counted again and found he had two putters and a total of fifteen clubs. Moments later, Joe Inman's caddie ran back from the first green. Joe had a short birdie putt but no putter. Both Inman and Eichelberger had identical black Callaway bags. Joe's putter was mistakenly put in Dave's bag. It almost cost both players.

After winning the Senior Open, Dave told the media, "I won because of him (me)." I smiled.

4

The Introduction

FIRST, LET ME SET THE RECORD STRAIGHT ON SOMETHING ATTRIBUTED TO ME. It was not I who introduced Bernhard Langer with a malaprop. It happened at The Players Championship, I am told. The starter obviously became confused and said the name "Long Hard Banger." After that, I was very careful in introducing Bernhard.

It was important, both to me and to the players, to say players' names and hometowns correctly. We went to exhaustive lengths to be 100 percent accurate.

When there was any question at all, a player was asked at registration to pronounce his name and hometown so that it was spoken correctly on the first tee. If there was any doubt, pronunciations were noted. That information was circulated to the media center and all TV commentators.

Some names were tricky. Frank Nobilo was one. His name appeared simple enough. When I asked, he said "NO-bil-lo." Announcers didn't buy it, saying "Nobil-lo" instead. During the broadcast, David Fay called me. "Are you sure it's NO-bil-lo?"

"Yes," I said. "Frank told me, 'You and my mom are the only ones who say it right. It's NO-bil-lo.' " David quickly spread the word. Five minutes later, announcers were saying it correctly.

In twenty-three years, my biggest challenge was the introduction of Jose Maria Olazabal. I cornered him before his start at Hazeltine in 1991. We had what appeared to be a private conversation, though eighteen hundred people were in a grandstand nearby.

"How do you say your name, and do I have to say the town?" I asked.

I was petrified.

"In Spanish, we combine Jose-Maria and say 'Chema.' " That made no sense to me.

"My last name is O-la-THA-bull."

I rehearsed "C-h-e-m-a….O-la-THA-bull" four times. He approved.

"As for the city, let's forget it, OK? I'll just say 'Spain,' " I said. Fuenterrabia was way above my Spanish vocabulary, which was limited to Cerveza brands.

"No, no, no, no," he insisted.

"Por favor, please let me quit while I'm ahead," I pleaded.

I suddenly felt the need to take a restroom break. Another USGA staffer, Mike Davis, or longtime USGA committeeman Tom O'Toole Jr., was always anxiously ready and close nearby to fill in for me if needed, and I was sure either could handle my new best friend's starting time with my send-off wishes of "Good luck."

But I plodded on.

"Foo-en-tu-rrrrrrr-bee-u," he kept saying. On my sixth attempt, he smiled. It was game time, and it was the U.S. Open. There were no mulligans.

"Ladies and gentlemen," I nervously began. "From Fooo-en-tu-rrrrrrrr-bee-u, Spain, Chema O-la-THA-bull." The microphone even picked up my sigh of relief.

The applause was resounding. My private tutorial had been overheard.

Before hitting, Chema turned, smiled and gave me a thumbs-up. In all the years, no introduction felt better.

Foreign names and cities were most challenging. I tried to say them as players pronounced them, not in an Americanized form. An example is Louie Oosthuizen of South Africa. TV announcers say OOST-hay-zen That's easy. Louis says WUUUST-hy-zuhn. I pronounced his name the way he did.

Miguel Angel Jimenez was a challenge for me. The amigo coached me, "Me-GALL…ON-hell…he-MEN-ez" was easy. I struggled more with his hometown—Malaga. It came out mu-LAG-a before I finally got it right—MAL-a-ga.

For all those years on the first tee, I announced the foreign cities of their homes, as was done for all Americans. Today, starters have eliminated foreign cities. It is not for me to wonder why.

Of course, when people see you trying your best to get foreign names right, they want you to make the announcement with a proper flair.

Two USGA colleagues, Tony Zirpoli and Rich Skyzinski, both lamented an introduction of Italy's Costantino Rocca.

"Put some Italian in it," they'd say. "It's not just 'Rocca.' Anyone can say it that way. Roll the R's. It's Rrrrrrrrrocca!"

Players became sensitive at times. Colin Montgomerie was emphatic in reminding his name was Colin, not Colon. Ian Woosnam made sure I said "Woos-nam." Somebody introduced him as Woos-man. Gotcha!

The player was always right.

I struggled with only one U.S. place name—Massachusetts. It was a mouthful.

* * *

During my last U.S. Open first-tee appearance in 2010, NBC's Steve Sands interviewed me on the first tee one morning. He said I was the only person who could say every letter in a name. Steve's comment seemed instructive to me.

"I'll change," I said.

Steve fired back, "No, no, no. That's a compliment. Don't change." That was flattering, coming from a true broadcasting pro.

My assignments never included being a starter at a women's event. That was a good thing. I'm not sure how long it might have taken me to master Virada Nira-pathpongporn.

5

The U.S. Open vs. The Open

THERE WERE DIFFERENCES IN STARTING PROTOCOL AT THE U.S. OPEN and The Open Championship (also known in layman's terms as the British Open).

Club count was one. Ivor Robson, a longtime first-tee starter for the Royal & Ancient's most well-known championship, didn't offer that reminder to players.

Second was the handling of scorecards. I made certain no player kept his own scorecard. Ivor did things differently. He gave scorecards to the players and let them shuffle the cards. Hopefully, no player had his own card. Unfortunately, that happened, once.

Mark Roe and Jesper Parnevik forgot to exchange scorecards at the 2003 Open at Royal St. George's in England. They were disqualified.

The third difference in protocol for the two Opens was the actual player introductions. I will forever hear Ivor's high-pitched voice saying, "This is game 24 . . . from USA . . . Tiger Woods."

I kept my introductions simple, too, but a few times, they were not always foolproof. Some of my gaffes are shared elsewhere, even causing me now to laugh.

6

My Last Words

MY FINAL PLAYER INTRODUCTIONS WERE AT PEBBLE BEACH IN 2010. "Ladies and gentlemen, this is the final pairing in the 110th United States Open Championship. The players are Dustin Johnson of Myrtle Beach, South Carolina, and Graeme McDowell of Portrush, Northern Ireland. Mr. Johnson has the honor. Play away, please."

After they were on their way up the first fairway, my smart phone buzzed. It was an e-mail from Hugh Burrows, a minister in Roswell, New Mexico, who wrote, "In Celtic, it's mick-DOE-el."

My career as first-tee starter had begun with a minor blip in 1986. I guess it ended with one, too.

7

Fuzzy Zoeller and Hubert Green: They Did What?

IT WAS MY SECOND DAY ON THE JOB AS A STARTER AT THE U.S. OPEN. Nineteen eighty-six. After a challenging first day—my rookie appearance with horrendous weather—Round Two was better. I was more prepared for anything. Or so I thought.

The pairings read Fuzzy Zoeller, Hubert Green, and Jerry Pate—three former U.S. Open champions going off at 1:00 P.M. I already knew Jerry had withdrawn because of an injury. That left jokesters Fuzzy and Hubert. They were buddies on the course but were more fun off the course. Their friendship always spilled over to the nineteenth hole.

When they arrived five minutes early on the first tee, I should have known they were up to something.

First, they ragged on Jerry (in Jerry's absence) about withdrawing. Their abuse, really, was all in fun.

Then I made a big mistake. I turned my back on these fun-loving scoundrels. The gallery lining the first hole began laughing uproariously. Fuzzy and Hubert were pulling a prank.

Fuzzy and Hubert each had a U.S. Open tee marker in hand, and they were marching to the forward tees.

Because of the lightheartedness, it seemed, for the moment, more like the Bing Crosby National Pro-Am, not the U.S. Open.

Once again, I was not in control. I decided to play along, yelling, "Security!" The gallery was loving it. Everybody was having fun.

Suddenly, the seriousness of their mischievous act hit me. There was the matter of the *Rules of Golf.* Competitors cannot change the course during play. If they do, they are disqualified. I was not in the mood to disqualify two former Open winners.

What happens if they deface the course *before* play?

I weighed the circumstance. It struck me as a no-harm, no-foul situation. Play had not yet begun, so the tee markers easily could be replaced in their original position. White dots painted on the grass during course setup indicated exactly where they were to go.

So, I retrieved the markers from the two clowns and replaced them precisely on the white dots.

In retrospect, I probably should have called P. J. Boatwright Jr. That decision, however, ran a risk. If the matter was brought to the attention of the Committee, who knows how long it might take to get an answer? Further, there was an embarrassment factor, both to the USGA and two former Open champions.

After Fuzzy and Hubert left the first tee. I sighed.

That evening, after the round was over, P. J. and I were enjoying a cocktail. P. J. was in good spirits. I brought up the Fuzzy-Hubert caper. I explained what they'd done.

P. J. was smoking his pipe, as always.

"They did *what*?" the dean of all rules officials asked.

He almost bit the end of his pipe.

After another drink, he had calmed.

Then he gave me one order: "Don't let that happen again."

Several years later, the *Rules of Golf* Committee wrote a Decision on players changing the course, as Fuzzy and Hubert had done. Since the players had not yet started the first hole, players were not penalized. I breathed a second sigh.

8

2005: Please Retrieve
Not the Ball but the Governor

I T FINALLY FELT LIKE THE U.S. OPEN. It was steamy hot in Round Two on Friday afternoon. Crowds were huge, and it seemed that at least a hundred of the spectators
were on the first tee and inside the ropes. Marshals had lost control. Spectators milled
everywhere. It was chaotic. I, too, had lost complete control.

There was good reason for the throng. Tiger Woods was about to play.

Everybody wanted a peek—a good peek.

Something had to be done, so I summoned three North Carolina state police
officers assigned there.

"We've got to get everybody out, back behind the ropes," I explained. "Everybody!"

The officers pulled it off. It didn't take long.

Then I learned we had done too good a job.

We had rushed the governor of North Carolina—Mike Easley—off the tee, too.
I had no idea Gov. Easley was in the audience. If I didn't correct the situation quickly,
they might hustle me off the tee, too.

"Officers, please find the governor and escort him back."

Tiger was ready to play.

Thankfully, they found the governor and brought him back to the starter's tent.
We cordially met, and I apologized. After sending Tiger down the first fairway, I gave

Gov. Easley a number of things in my stockpile of materials: a copy of the *Rules of Golf*, *The Decisions on The Rules of Golf*, pairing sheets, an official scorecard, a hole-location sheet, the "Notice to Competitors," a souvenir U.S. Open pencil, and a handful of Open tees. I never did learn if he even played golf.

9

The No. 1 Question

"WHO ARE THE NICEST PLAYERS?" That's a tough question to answer and one that I was asked often through the years. The list would be long, but I was lucky. I got to interact with players on the first tee when most were smiling.

Tony Zirpoli, a close associate for many years, had a tougher assignment. He was the official in the scoring area. He dealt with players after their struggles over eighteen holes. If we each compiled a list of the nicest players, the names we would each select would be different.

I will say this. None were nicer than gentlemen such as Gil Morgan, Dan Forsman, Jay Haas, and Steve Stricker, but there were many others. The list of those who were difficult was very short.

Gil Morgan was unique. He always thanked me before leaving the first tee. His kindness became so customary that I later wagered a dollar with referees who accompanied his group that he would thank me. Yes, I won a few bucks, but I never collected.

But "nicest" was not the No. 1 question I was ever asked.

"Did you ever use the restroom while on the first tee?"

Honestly, that question has been posed a thousand times.

The question was prompted by the lore of abstinence by Ivor Robson, the R&A's starter at The Open Championship for forty-one years. It was said Ivor never left his post on the first tee.

Ivor and I met only once, briefly, on the first tee of the Old Course at St. Andrews in 2000. It didn't seem appropriate to ask his secret.

I did observe Ivor in 2010, again at the home of golf. It might have been a moment of history. He disappeared from the first tee for a short time before the introduction of Graeme McDowell. My hunch is he was only getting a snack.

Here's the answer to my No. 1 question:

Yes, I did take a few breaks. I was no Ivor.

10

1999: When Jumbo Wouldn't Budge

R OUNDS ONE AND TWO USUALLY BEGAN AT 7 A.M., BUT IN 1999 AT PINEHURST, IT WAS DIFFERENT. It was decided that play would start at 6:30, hoping the field of 156 would complete play before darkness arrived Thursday evening.

I arrived at the first tee before 6 A.M. A flashlight was required.

After setting up the starter's box, I found the tee markers. Something was strange. Upon further examination, it was clear the markers were not pointed properly down the first fairway. They were aimed slightly to the right, toward the eighteenth fairway. Tom Meeks, already out doing course set-up, had placed them in total darkness, before my arrival.

It was not my normal responsibility to touch the markers. The only time I ever did was when pranksters Fuzzy Zoeller and Hubert Green moved the markers at Shinnecock Hills.

I called Tom to explain the issue. He instructed me to correct the problem and then to paint a fresh white dot to indicate the new location. I did as ordered.

I got down on hands and knees in the dark to "erase" the old white dot he had sprayed. The mission was accomplished minutes before the first group arrived at 6:25. Brandel Chamblee and David Toms appeared, eager to play. Jumbo Ozaki finally showed, and he was not happy.

I had a dilemma—actually, two problems.

First, the rules official assigned to accompany the group was AWOL. We scrambled, and staffer Tony Zirpoli agreed to fill in, at least temporarily. Tony sprinted to the first tee to assume referee duties. He was breathless, but ready. So, one problem was solved.

Tony aided in solving problem number two.

At precisely 6:30, I began the introductions.

"Ladies and gentlemen," I said. "This is the 6:30 starting time. Please welcome, from Chiba, Japan, Jumbo Ozaki. Play away, please."

Jumbo just stood there, looking like an oak tree, refusing to move.

Even in the darkness, he was a big man, not the size of a sumo wrestler, but he could probably handle himself against one. He owned a clothing line and was wearing a shirt perhaps more suitable on Halloween or in a Fellini movie. The shirt seemed to glow. In the morning darkness, we needed his glow.

"I won't play," he said in Japanese.

This was a new problem for me and one for which I was unprepared.

I looked at Tony and said, "What do I do now?"

"Start him," Tony said.

Jumbo and I huddled. Three times I asked him to play. He refused, saying that he could not see the fairway. Our stand-off lasted several minutes.

Brandel credited my diplomacy for cajoling Jumbo to finally play. The truth is, I pleaded.

He was the first and only to ever receive a re-introduction.

"From Chiba, Japan . . . Jumbo Ozaki. Play away, please," and this time I emphasized *please*.

He teed slowly, waiting for the light fog to clear and for the slightest bit of additional daylight. When he finally drove, flashbulbs went off inside and outside the ropes. Japanese cameramen were everywhere—on the first tee and in the drive zone, attempting to capture photos of their star. Actually, their light might have helped.

David Toms was next. He did so in his usual agreeable way. So did Brandel. Off they went with Tony. The additional time helped him catch his breath.

There was an interesting aspect to their play in Rounds One and Two. Brandel and David were not known as long hitters, but on Thursday, they drove within proximity to Jumbo, who was recognized as one of the game's longest.

In Friday's Round Two, things changed. Jumbo outdrove the Americans by fifty yards throughout the round. Maybe Jumbo had recovered from jet lag.

Or perhaps he was experiencing a renewed happiness in playing at a more reasonable hour.

11

The Start of My
U.S. Open Experience

ONE PERSON CALLED HIM PURVIS. To most, he was Mr. Boatwright. For those fortunate to know him, he was simply P. J. In the world of golf, he was recognized as the game's foremost authority on the *Rules of Golf*.

P. J. mentored many. I could name a dozen. Though I was among the last, he shaped my forty-three years in serving the game.

Our relationship began in 1972. It was at Pebble Beach, the first U.S. Open held there. It was also my first Open.

There was much for me to learn before ever thinking about working on golf's biggest stage. In fact, the thought of playing any role at the U.S. Open never entered my mind. However, I was eager to learn more about conducting championship golf.

Shortly before the 1972 Open, I was given the opportunity to take a baby step in my learning process. With my less than two years' experience at the Northern California Golf Association, Bob Hanna, the NCGA executive director, assigned me to be a rules official at the Northern California PGA's stroke play championship. It was my first opportunity to actually apply the rules. I was to be the head official on a committee of one—me. I had read the *Rules of Golf* on rainy days in our offices above the ninth green at Spyglass Hill, but I had no practical experience in interpreting the rules or in dealing with players under pressure. My eagerness was met with apprehension, which, as I learned many years later, is the same feeling every rules official has the first few tournaments they work. Until you're called upon to act, you're scared to death.

The tournament was at the new Rancho Murieta Golf Club near Sacramento. On the first day, I was under a tree, hiding, hoping nobody would find me, much less ask me to decide an important rules issue. I was reading the *Rules of Golf,* perhaps for the tenth time.

Then came my worst fear. I was being hailed.

The request did not come from just any player. It came from a former U.S. Open champion. He was the only one I recognized in the field of club pros. The player was Jack Fleck, the man who defeated Ben Hogan in a playoff in the 1955 U.S. Open at The Olympic Club. His shout was a frightening moment.

"Why does he want me?" I wondered as I rumbled off in my cart. Once face to face with him, I learned he did not need rules expertise after all.

"Young man," he barked, "take me in."

He was quitting the competition after only five holes.

We did not speak on our ride to the parking lot. I was too scared. As we neared the lot, I looked for the biggest car, probably a Cadillac, I surmised. Certainly every U.S. Open champion drove one!

Instead, I was directed to a little red car. In a matter of seconds, Fleck removed his heavy bag from the cart, popped the trunk and thrust his Hogan clubs into it, quite forcefully, followed by even greater energy given to the door.

Jack Fleck was my first "trunk slammer." He was not the last.

As I'd realize over the years, that experience became helpful in dealing with some U.S. Open contestants.

Over the next few days, I made several rules decisions. All were accurate and nonconfrontational.

Well, one was confrontational.

Shortly after my encounter with Fleck, pro Ben Doyle wanted free relief from grass clippings piled about a hundred yards from play and under the same tree under which I had hidden earlier. Free relief was denied. Ben held a friendly grudge for the next four decades.

This PGA event was a solidly grounded stepping stone. It taught me that rules officials could gain respect and even friendships while upholding the rules. That lesson lasted, and I was ready to learn more, even at the U.S. Open.

A few months later, I attended a special 1972 U.S. Open dinner at The Lodge at Pebble Beach. It was Wednesday evening before the first round.

Mr. Boatwright was at the head table, among dignitaries. I was awed. We had never met, though I had watched Boatwright referee the 1963 U.S. Amateur final at Wakonda Club, where I worked while attending Drake University. He still had the aura of nine years earlier. He was respected by everyone around him. In the nineteen years I knew him, that respect only grew.

I had a question for P. J. that evening, a personal request. As I approached to introduce myself, I felt the same nervousness as my encounter with Jack Fleck.

"Mr. Boatwright," I said, "may I accompany you to cut the holes in the morning?"

Clearly, my interest did not excite him.

I do not recall his exact response, but a chain of huddled meetings ensued. He first went to Frank "Sandy" Tatum, chairman of the Championship. Sandy then spoke with Lynford Lardner Jr., president of the USGA. Sandy and I were acquainted, and he must have convinced Lardner, who granted approval. P. J's orders were to observe only. He instructed me to meet him at 5 A.M. I did not need an alarm clock. I awaited my new mentor in darkness on the first tee.

As with Fleck, I didn't say a word.

P. J. had a well-organized plan for the location of each hole. At No. 1, his notes indicated a "back right" location, roughly twenty paces from the front and five from the right. (Five paces was P. J's minimum from the green's edge. Today, the guideline is no less than three yards.) P. J's distances were not precise, as done with a tape measure now. Paces were strides, and his was one yard, or close enough. P. J. was the standard.

On Thursday morning, greens were already as firm as cart paths, and their grass was more gray than green in color. P. J. had already painted a white dot on each green the previous afternoon in order to locate holes for the grounds crew the next morning. He put a white paint can on the dot, then putted several balls from every direction at the can. To him, the most important putt was downhill to see if balls might roll considerable distance beyond the hole. He was a good putter, reminding me of legendary pro Jackie Burke,Jr. He usually tapped the white can with most putts. Each location was what P. J. liked to call "competitive"—difficult, but fair. The location selected was reasonably flat, without severe break, within two feet of the white can. When satisfied, he instructed the hole-cutter to cut the hole on the exact spot he had put the can. The hole-cutter was the only person to accompany us. P. J. did not need a committee on this exercise; he *was* the committee.

He set tees and cut holes in sequential order, starting at 1 and proceeding in order to 18. Course set-up usually took about three hours.

Tee markers were five to seven paces apart. He sometimes widened blocks slightly on the par-3s, like at Pebble Beach's old par-3 fifth—uphill, out of bounds right, lateral hazard left, and a treacherous green. The old hole was brutal, usually playing over par, and selection of the hole was often the hardest on the course.

Along the way at Pebble Beach, P. J. shared some of his methodology with me. Before the Open, he gave each green his expert thought. He did so from his desk at Golf House. He didn't use typography maps. He plotted general location for each hole of the four rounds. Holes for practice rounds were not near those he selected for the Championship. Because greens at Pebble Beach are relatively small, hole selection there is not easy.

Before arriving at the Open, he assigned a rating of 1, 2, 3, or 4 to each hole location of the four Championship rounds. For example, if he had chosen the four easiest locations on a day, the total rating difficulty would have been 18 (1 x 18). If he had picked four hardest holes, the rating would have been 72 (4 x 18). He never selected those combinations—all 1s or all 4s. His goal was a rating of 42 every day. Each round had an approximate balance of 1s, 2s, 3s and 4s each day. The total was 42 every day. Holes were "U.S. Open difficult" each round, but they were always fair. He did not believe in setting up the course easy Thursday and then become progressively more difficult each day.

I was learning from the best, and we were only on the front nine that Thursday. P. J. was antsy when we arrived at No. 10. It was 6:30 A.M. and the sun was rising over the Monterey Peninsula. Many of the 156 caddies were already walking the course, pacing yardages, learning precisely where P. J. placed the holes and, frankly, they were getting in the way of his work. That bothered him. Also annoying was the crowd that was gathering. Early spectators had found a semi-hidden path leading from Carmel Beach to the tenth green, thus avoiding buying tickets. With play beginning in about thirty minutes, P. J. needed to get back to the first tee for the start. Later, he would return to finish the course set-up—alone.

Of course, this was an era when all the players started their rounds at No. 1. More recently, it has become commonplace to start players at both 1 and 10 on the first two days, but in 1972, P. J. knew it would be a few hours before any players got to the second nine.

Now he said, "Ronny, do you see where I put the white dot on the green?"

He pointed to a back-left position on the tenth green. This time, he took a white tee and with considerable effort, he stuck the tee into the green. That act took considerable effort.

"Yes, sir," I responded. Those may have been my first words that morning.

"Cut the hole right there." The man trusted me. I went from "five-eleven to about six-three," P. J.'s height.

Then he drove off, taking the white can with him and leaving his apprentice hole-placer behind.

I watched that tee he had punched into the hard surface like the tee was the Cullinan Diamond. I did not blink for five minutes.

The hole-cutter was still on the ninth green, delayed a bit by a new U.S. Open procedure to paint the inside of the hole by hand. The hole-cutter also double-checked each flagstick to see that it stood as perfectly vertical as possible. All this took time.

While waiting, I realized my ride was gone, and No. 10 green was the farthest point on the course. I had a thought. The gallery marshal nearby was going to the first tee. I seized the opportunity for a ride. He agreed to take me, but first, the hole had to be cut.

I made a poor decision. I delegated the one responsibility assigned to me. It was a hasty decision, one regretted to this day.

A security guard was behind the green. He was trying to stop the flood of Carmel beachcombers sneaking into the U.S. Open.

"Sir, could you help me, please?" I asked.

"Uh, sure," he said. He was perplexed by the flow of spectators ignoring his orders to stop. He was losing badly.

"When the hole-cutter arrives, make certain he cuts the hole right there!" I instructed. "Got it?"

He nodded, yes. From his look, I was certain he didn't play golf, and he probably had never seen a tee. He had no idea the importance of his new role. Frankly, neither did I. Later that day, I learned.

Off I rode with the gallery marshal, leaving the security guard to perform the critical job P. J. had assigned me.

Thursday was a windy day, one difficult for golf. Five players broke par, scoring 71, 1 under par. Jack Nicklaus, the eventual champion, was one. Gary Player scored 72 and Tony Jacklin, the defending champion, scored 75.

Gary and Tony complained to P. J. about one hole location. Guess which one.

"Did you cut the tenth hole where I told you?" P. J. asked.

"Yes, it was," I said, obviously not 100 percent certain of my answer. With guilt nagging, I made the long walk to No. 10. The horde that had snuck into the Open were now headed back to Carmel Beach. They watched me on hands and knees, this time, looking at the hole. I looked for any evidence, even the tiny hole left by that white tee. I could not find it. That was a good sign. I was sure the hole location was exactly where P. J. had intended.

I found P. J. and confirmed my finding.

"Yes, sir, No. 10 was precisely where you instructed." I did not share the rest of the story.

That evening, our dog, Prince Beau, bit legendary San Francisco sports writer Art Spander. Round 1 did not seem my day.

Brighter times were ahead. I worked with P. J. at eighteen national championships—eleven Opens, two Senior Opens, the Women's Open, a U.S. Amateur, and three Women's Amateurs.

At the 1984 Women's Amateur, P. J. did something that earned my eternal respect.

We were enjoying ourselves at the Players' Dinner at Seattle's Broadmoor Golf Club when someone at Golf House headquarters in Far Hills, New Jersey, called. Golf professionals in Niagara Falls, New York, and Detroit, Michigan, needed help. It was very late there.

Pros in each city wanted rules decisions. Depending upon how the USGA ruled, they might have to disqualify their own members. It was serious stuff. Pride, prizes, and maybe even the jobs of these pros were at stake.

I explained the circumstances to P. J., who then asked for my opinion. To my great relief, he concurred with my conclusions, based on the Decisions of Golf. He had that confidence in me. That was a gold medal moment.

"Ronny, call them back and tell them our decisions."

It was the first time I realized the power of the USGA. Its decision was final. It was as though we were the Supreme Court of Golf, though perhaps more importantly, personally, I had earned the confidence of P. J. Boatwright Jr.

Only those who ever worked with P. J. will understand exactly what having his confidence meant. It was a gold medal, never seen, but one worn forever.

In the 1984 Open at Winged Foot Golf Club, outside New York City, P. J. again showed his confidence in me. Round One was under way, and early players were headed to the back nine holes when P. J. called. He was panicked, something not often witnessed. It was contrary to his relaxed, Southern nature.

"Ronny, get some red paint and come out to No. 15 as fast as you can!"

"Yes, sir," I responded. I had no idea why P. J. needed me.

The request was easier ordered than accomplished. First, I had to find red paint hiding somewhere at Winged Foot's thirty-six-hole facility. I also had to find a paint-spray gun. Then I had to find a golf cart. Finally, the drive from the clubhouse to the fifteenth hole was blocked by what seemed to be all of the thirty thousand spectators in my path. Somehow, I found a circuitous route through the golf being played and the throng. It took about an hour.

When I finally arrived, P. J. was near a boundary fence with arms crossed. His demeanor read, "What took you so long?"

Two others were there: Betsy Rawls, three-time U.S. Women's Open champion, and Jack Tuthill. Betsy and Jack were the respective heads of rules for the LPGA and PGA Tours. If there were a hall of fame of rules officials, this threesome should be its first inductees.

"Ronny, we've found a lateral water hazard back here," P. J. said. "Paint it—fast! Here come golfers."

Everybody had to play the same U.S. Open set-up, so time was critical.

How did this ditch escape P. J.'s attention during his many visits to Winged Foot? It puzzled me, but this was no time to ask.

I removed the top of the paint can and fitted the can into the paint gun. Luckily, I did not spray red paint on my pants or shoes—a first. In the presence of rules all-stars, I was feeling the pressure of this simple task as golfers neared.

I inched along, spraying red paint, knowing the eyes of three experts were watching closely. The red line may have been the straightest ever painted. The first group had yet to arrive. All three smiled.

A year later, I was in the company of another elite group of rules officials—P. J., Tuthill, David Eger, and Joe "Mac" England. This was at the annual USGA meeting in Boston.

Mac was P. J.'s longtime friend, and he was probably the only person who could hold his own in any rules debate with the world's expert. I had a question for this august group.

"Have you ever made a rules mistake?" The question struck a nerve. A lively, convivial discussion followed. One by one, each confessed, admitting to a variety of errors. P. J. went last.

"No, can't say that I have!" P. J. proclaimed.

Mac England piled on, relating several of P. J.'s mistakes. He raised one incident that was well publicized.

At the 1981 U.S. Open at Merion, P. J. assessed a two-stroke penalty on Forrest Fezler and John Schroeder for undue delay—or what everyone knows as slow play. They finished twenty minutes late. Schroeder appealed and P. J.'s decision was overruled by the Rules Committee. This stung him at the time, but he now laughed.

I dared not bring up his "undue delay" in finding that water hazard at Winged Foot.

* * *

Reflecting on what P. J. Boatwright Jr. meant to golf and to me, several thoughts are clear. He was not a man of many words, nor was he one to endorse changes to the game. I am confident he would abhor the commercialism that has crept into golf, as well as the advances of technology. They would not have gained a foothold with him.

His goal at the U.S. Open was simple—to identify the best golfer in the game. He tested abilities under pressure, usually finding the weaknesses of many, both in their abilities and attitudes. He wanted players to use every club in their bags. He wanted them to hit drivers to narrow fairways not ever exceeding thirty yards in width and often less. He was not obsessed with a concern of today—"taking the driver out of players' hands."

He never set up a 280-yard par 3, and the only drivable par-4s—common today—were Hole 6 at Winged Foot and Hole 17 at Oakmont. His par-5s were rarely reached, and if a player tried and missed, he often paid a severe price.

The idea of alternating tees—long one day and short the next—never entered his mind. His mindset was bold: "Here's the hole. Prepare for the challenge. Have at it."

He did acquiesce once. After years of pestering, he finally created a chipping area. This one area took the place of deep rough around greens. He tiptoed into this change, first trying it behind the fourteenth green at the 1992 Open at Pebble Beach. I credit another P. J.—Peter Jacobsen, for suggesting it. Jake's idea caught on, and P. J. used chipping areas—occasionally.

He had a reverence for par—on each hole and for the championship over seventy-two holes. Any player who arrived at the U.S. Open could target even par over four rounds and know with reasonable certainty he would be a serious contender.

P. J. had two defenses to protect par—severe rough and firm greens. He ordered two levels of grass: short and tall. Fairways were short, rewarding iron shots crisply struck. Rough was severe and dense, leveled at about six inches with Bermuda rough at four inches. Greens were firm. A ball could be heard hitting the green. He wanted a well-hit iron to skip forward once, maybe twice, then stop.

Rarely would iron shots spin backward, like today. His deep rough did not reward shots landing on firm greens, and recovery from rough for par was possible, but improbable. He intended that rough would be a one-half stroke penalty. Sometimes, the penalty was more.

In 1986, Scott Williams tried to play safely off the first tee at Shinnecock Hills. He hit a four-wood but missed the fairway by inches. When he finally found the ball after a search of four minutes and fifty-eight seconds, Scott took a penalty for an unplayable lie, adding one stroke. Some might think Scott's predicament was unfair for such a narrowly missed, slightly errant shot. Not P. J. One hundred fifty-six golfers faced the same challenge, and he was only attempting to identify the best of them. He demanded the champion hit fairways and greens.

More than once, in a most Southern drawl, he said, "Who says, bigga is betta?"

To P. J., that meant several things. Knowing him, the comment applied to any change that might threaten the game, and he saw his role to act as guardian of golf's most challenging examination. He did it better than anyone.

P. J. Boatwright Jr. was a mentor in many ways. After eleven U.S. Opens, he was also my friend.

By the way, the only man who ever called him Purvis was Mac.

12

Another Mentor: Frank Hannigan

CASUAL DRESS WAS HIS SIGNATURE: KHAKIS, WHITE SHIRT—AND NO TIE. More formal attire, like the blue blazer with the association's "flying chicken" emblem, as ABC TV privately dubbed it, was for others.

Frank Hannigan was "good company" in any company—from Augusta National Golf Club to public courses on Staten Island, where he grew up. He preferred the munis, where he could put golf shoes on in the parking lot. He had no pretension. He laughed a lot and he made others laugh with his rare wit.

My earliest remembrance of Frank was a note to me in 1972. It was early in my time at the Northern California Golf Association. He had received a letter from Broderick, California containing a question on the rules. The Broderick postmark caught Frank's attention. He asked me if the town was named after U.S. Senator David Broderick. Frank knew history—American and golf. It was Senator Broderick who had squared off against David Terry, the state's chief justice. Their contest was not a debate or an election. They hated each other, stemming from differences over abolition of slavery. They settled the matter with pistols on September 13, 1859. Three days later, Broderick died from injuries sustained in what was the last duel in the U.S.

The duel took place near what is now the seventh hole at San Francisco Golf Club.

Setting history aside, the crux of the letter from Broderick was another serious dispute. The outcome would decide a $1 Nassau wager.

Two former golf pals were not speaking while they awaited Frank's decision.

One had conceded a short putt to the other, his opponent. The opponent ignored the concession and putted anyway. He missed. They argued. Was the putt good, or because it was missed, was it a failed effort? The matter became contentious. Frank joked that the match should be decided like Senator Broderick and Justice Terry—with a duel.

Frank shared with me the answer he would send to Broderick, Calif.: Rule 2-4 said, "A concession may not be declined or withdrawn." The putt was good. The hole was over. Gun shots would not be fired.

Frank's wit was always scissors sharp. To him, "Green grass is for cemeteries." He favored an off-color-look, indicating the turf's dryness and ground's firmness. Greens were too fast today because of the Stimpmeter and modern turf practices.

He admonished, saying, "Slow grass is better than fast dirt." He described senior golf with large purses as, "Social Security for senior golfers." During his five years as the USGA's executive director, he dealt with a board of fifteen. He shared a pragmatic philosophy, privately, for keeping his job, "Make sure you have eight votes." And after many years of arranging golf for others, he dumped that thankless task on me with, "I don't do golf."

He may not have "done" golf, but he "got" golf. To him, golf was always a game, played 99.999 percent of the time by amateurs. He hypothesized that if the great earthquake along the San Andreas Fault struck during the old Bing Crosby Clambake, causing the Monterey Peninsula to fall into the Pacific Ocean, there would be thirty million amateurs on the U.S. mainland still enjoying golf. The foundation of Frank's game was amateur golf and those who played only for fun. He was a populist, and, to him, amateur golfers were bigger than the stars we celebrate.

Some thought he lacked diplomacy and was perhaps abrupt. At times, maybe he was. Frank was a no-nonsense leader and those around him knew exactly where he stood, much like P. J. We trusted both implicitly.

Frank's management style was unique. He surrounded himself with golf people, those passionate about serving golf, like himself. The USGA was a nonprofit, charitable organization, and our compensation came second to our mission.

He delegated assignments and kept instructions minimal. He was not effusive in expressing gratitude for the long and dedicated hours. His team never required praise.

I worked with Frank at many national championships. In the first three events, we were a total staff of two, Frank and me, running the events. We did everything, setting up the course for play in darkness at 5:00 A.M., then locking the office door in moonlight after calling newspapers and magazines around the U.S. with the day's results. We still managed to have fun. We probably accomplished what ten do today. To him, bigger was not necessarily better, just like P. J. Perhaps that reflected Frank's frugality.

We teamed first at the 1975 U.S. Senior Amateur at Carmel Valley Country Club, near Carmel, California. Frank refereed the final match, riding in a golf cart. At the fifth hole, Bill Colm hit an errant shot that was destined for a lake, but the ball never got there. It landed in Frank's cart. A humbled Hannigan took responsibility. He had impacted the match. He decreed immediately that referees would no longer ride; they would walk, as required by the players. The Hannigan Rule remains in effect today.

His judgment was usually considered golf law. I learned that fact at my first USGA Executive Committee meeting in 1982. The board proposed that amateurs could play for cash prizes equaling the value of merchandise awards—then $500.

Frank simply proclaimed, "We're not doing that." He found more than eight votes and the proposal was withdrawn. Cash prizes remained prohibited. The PGA of America breathed a sigh. Frank's staff did, too.

* * *

In 1983, Frank left a semi-retirement status with USGA to succeed Harry Easterly as executive director. Early on, he persuaded the USGA to take the U.S. Open to Shinnecock Hills, site of the first Open in 1895.

The U.S. Open had outgrown Shinnecock Hills' ability to fully organize it. Frank committed his staff to manage everything.

He assigned Tony Zirpoli to head the effort. Tony had the credentials. First, he was a Long Islander who "spoke the language," and he got along with everybody.

Critical in that relationship was Superintendent Pete Smith, chief of the Shinnecock Indian tribe that maintained the course. Tony occasionally, and figuratively, smoked a "peace pipe" with the Shinnecock Tribe when issues became heated. He also coerced the county to fund a walking bridge over busy Highway 27, which ran right by the club's entrance. His effort on that bridge was a nongolf stroke of genius. Hannigan's gamble at Shinnecock paid dividends later. It paved the way for all future U.S. Opens organized, managed, and conducted by the USGA staff.

Frank gambled in another way at Shinnecock. A first-tee starter was needed. He and P. J. Boatwright, Jr. chose me. And, yes, Frank's instructions were few, and his sendoff was, "Welcome to show biz."

Naming me was not Frank's greatest achievement.

Fostering of the Mid-Amateur Championship was significant. He foresaw that college and young pre-professional golfers were dominating amateur golf. First, he tried to prohibit eligibility in the U.S. Amateur Public Links Championships. His rationale was simple: college kids had plenty of competitive golf opportunities, almost year 'round, at private and public courses. They paid for little—greens fees or equipment. A mid-amateur for golfers age twenty-five and older was his answer.

* * *

The issue Frank raised over the Public Links championships was easily solvable, but he did not have the eight votes to ban college golfers who had received grants-in-aid or competed on college teams. Only after Frank's death in 2014 did USGA drop the two events for public golfers. Had they eliminated the Publinks earlier, Frank's commentary—and his wrath—would have been good reading.

After leaving USGA in 1988, Frank joined ABC, offering expertise on the rules during the broadcasts of USGA championships.

In 1995, he and his wife, Janet, moved permanently to a retirement community in New York, described to me as a commune. From there, he opined in "Letters from Saugerties," from where he challenged the golf world about everything—rules, amateurism, college golf, and technology.

If Frank remained at the USGA, the advancement of technology with their commercial interests would have met its match under his leadership. In retirement, he had a tall soapbox and a love for golf, though his garden had taken priority. He was always an amateur at heart, but he was a professional at growing roses.

Frank loved basketball, too. When he passed away in April 2014, I'm sure he still had his NCAA brackets from that year's tournament. He was not a big gambler, but he studied betting lines, even in golf. He wore eyeshades to analyze every detail. He studied rankings, playing trends, and even the weather. His golf wagers were small, placed online in the U.K. He gave me a good tip on golf betting, "Take foreign players in early rounds of match play." No doubt he wagered on the Europeans in all Ryder Cups.

Frank Hannigan was considered once for the World Golf Hall of Fame. My bet is he was amused. If elected and if he chose to attend, his attendance would have been only to see two close friends, Judy Rankin and Peter Alliss. He wanted to visit the U.K. "one more time . . . to spend time with Peter."

* * *

I wrote Frank before his passing, expressing something not easy to convey—what he had meant personally to me and to our game. We spoke occasionally in his last years. I always pictured him with a phone, sitting in one of his beloved gardens or reading a good book in his study.

From those calls, it was clear. He never lost interest in what was best for the game of golf. We shared openly. Like with P. J., it was reassuring that we usually agreed.

In thirty-two years wandering the halls at Golf House, I never found Frank's portrait. I must not have looked hard enough because it now hangs with P. J. Boatwright Jr.— proteges of Joseph C. Dey. Together, they built what some called, "the finest organization in sports."

They did it putting on trousers "one leg at a time." Yes, Frank's khakis were always rumpled, his trademark. Admirers said he did his best thinking wearing them.

13

1992: This Open Almost Closed Before It Opened

HISTORY WILL FOREVER RECORD THAT THE 1992 U.S. OPEN WAS HELD AT PEBBLE BEACH AND THAT TOM KITE WAS THE WINNER. Not widely known is that both the site and its champion were in doubt from start to finish. Like fabled newscaster Paul Harvey would say, "Now—the rest of the story."

First, there was the question of the venue.

Japanese businessman Minoru Isutani purchased Pebble Beach Company from movie/oil mogul Marvin Davis in September 1990. Isutani would later encounter trouble, both from public relations and financial standpoints.

He quietly planned to sell memberships at Pebble Beach with preferred starting times. When that notion became known, the California Coastal Commission nixed the membership proposal. Isutani was also delinquent on property taxes at another golf course he owned, this one in Los Angeles. These issues made the USGA uncomfortable in moving forward with the U.S. Open at Pebble Beach.

In June 1991, about a year before that Pebble Beach Open would take place, USGA president C. Grant Spaeth, executive director David Fay, and I met to discuss all issues regarding the upcoming championship. We met at a little garden shop, outdoors, about one hundred feet from the Pebble Beach pro shop. Passersby had no idea of the historic significance of our gathering. I didn't, either.

The U.S. Open is the bedrock of the USGA's financial stability. Barring unforeseen circumstances, such as war, the Open has not been moved or cancelled. On this quiet occasion, however, we talked of moving the Open from this iconic site.

My role was that of having local intelligence, both as a longtime resident and USGA representative. I had been involved in organizational and contractual details of the U.S. Open at Pebble Beach nine years earlier, and I knew the "players" in the Pebble Beach organization going back to the 1972 Open.

I shared that PB had new owners—Sumitomo Bank and two of its subsidiaries. Isutani was gone, having been removed from ownership.

If there was a contingency, a Plan B plan to go elsewhere, we never discussed it at our garden meeting.

Given the assurances from our meeting, Spaeth convinced the Championship Committee to proceed with the Open at Pebble Beach the following June.

With the Open now firmly on course, Pebble Beach Company president Tom Oliver wrote to Spaeth on July 11, 1991, thanking Grant for his part in literally saving the Open there. With the deal, Oliver was effusive in his gratitude. He offered Pebble Beach for the 1994 U.S. Amateur, then added an invitation to host the 1998 U.S. Women's Open.

Later, both invitations for the Amateur and Women's Open were withdrawn in favor of one event—the 1999 U.S. Amateur. With catastrophe quietly avoided, the 1992 Open would proceed. We had only eleven months to pull it off.

That June week in 1992 was everything hoped for at Pebble Beach—bright skies and thick Open rough. In the end, Colin Montgomerie scored 70 on Sunday, the day's best round in windy conditions for which only a Scot, or maybe a Texan, might be comfortable. It looked like Montgomerie would claim the title until Jeff Sluman birdied 18 to pass Monty. In the end, though, a Texan prevailed. Steady Tom Kite's name was atop the scoreboard. Few knew the outcome was still in question. There was one matter yet to be settled.

A television viewer called the USGA. He hypothesized Kite had tapped down something other than a ball mark on the seventy-first hole. This created an unprecedented, serious moment in the scoring trailer. Officials David Eger and M. J. Mastalir huddled with the leader. Kite was very much aware of his actions on the green at 17. He immediately explained it was only a ball mark. A video validated his action. The suspenseful episode took about thirty seconds to resolve. Tom Kite, a man of impeccable integrity, emerged from the trailer smiling as the rightful winner. The win was especially sweet for Kite because it removed from him the albatross, the unofficial title of "Best Golfer Never to Have Won a Major."

What if a penalty had been assessed? That was not a public announcement I would have wanted to make.

And what if the 1992 Open had been moved from Pebble Beach? That, too, would have been a first. Thankfully, we'll never know how history might have changed. Opens at Pebble Beach in 2000, 2010, and 2019 have now followed.

In 2019, Pebble Beach was set to hold its sixth Open in the course's centennial year.

14

2007: Chaos and Levity at Oakmont

Today, there are those who won't stand for the national anthem. I'm not one, but it's their right.

My problem at Oakmont was to figure out how to get the people to sit down.

This might be one of those you-had-to-be-there stories.

For each of the first 101 U.S. Opens, every player started his round from hole 1. That tradition changed in 2002, when it was decided to start from both 1 and 10 in the first and second rounds at Bethpage State Park's Black Course. The idea was to shorten the golf day, increasing the likelihood of finishing before darkness because of the possibility of weather delays.

The split-tee format shortens the time for all 156 golfers to complete play. It also gives the Committee a bit more flexibility if bad weather causes any delay in play.

The two-tee system requires dividing the field of 156 into four groups of 39 players each. Two waves play in the morning, one starting at No. 1 and proceed in a normal fashion to 18, and the other begin at No. 10, playing the second nine holes first, and then Nos. 1-9. The process repeats in the afternoon.

That was the plan for the first round at Oakmont in 2007.

But something happened in the last group of players that started at No. 1 in the morning. It was unexpected, and I was ill-prepared.

In that group were Michael Berg of Detroit Lake, Minnesota, Jason Kokrak of Warren, Ohio, and Kyle Hobbs of Ann Arbor, Michigan.

Berg had the honor, and his three-metal found the left-center of the fairway. Next was Kokrak. Unfortunately, he pushed a drive far right, dangerously near out-of-bounds. The third player, Hobbs, split the fairway. Berg, Hobbs, and their caddies marched off the tee, not realizing Kokrak would be hitting a provisional ball for his errant tee shot. At the same time, thousands in the grandstands rose in unison.

I asked rules official Grover Walker, who was standing next to me, "Where are they going?"

Like Berg and Hobbs, we guessed spectators were not aware Kokrak was about to play another ball from the tee. Furthermore, fans in the grandstand at the first tee perhaps did not realize that if they stayed seated, they would soon see more golf. Players who started at the tenth hole were headed to the first hole for their second nine.

Amid the chaos, Kokrak tried to compose himself prior to playing a dreaded provisional ball. As he prepared, his fellow competitors were already in the fairway. Adding to the confusion was the noisy crowd, moving everywhere, some even leaving the grandstand. Kokrak didn't know what to do. Neither did I.

I had never faced this situation, nor was I prepared. In fairness to Jason, I had to try to gain control—quickly.

All I could think to shout into the microphone was, "Ladies and gentlemen . . . please stand!"

The command worked. There was immediate silence. Grover and I looked up to see everybody stop in place. Thousands were now standing at military attention. Men removed their hats and were placing them over their hearts. Grover and I were definitely not going to lead them in the National Anthem, but that's what it looked like.

When the noise subsided, I did not sing, but managed to say, "Mr. Kokrak, please play away."

Referee Walker laughed uncontrollably. So did I.

Pittsburgh's great fans had no trouble standing, even respectfully—for a provisional ball. They stand for the National Anthem, too.

15

Wanted: A Referee in the U.S. Open

T HE FIRST TEE WAS BADLY IN NEED. Rain had finally stopped on yet another start-and-stop day of golf at the 2009 U.S. Open at Bethpage Black, in Farmingdale, New York.

Jim Furyk, Paul Casey, and Geoff Ogilvy were present and ready to play. The players had their instructions, dry scorecards, hole-location sheets, and "Notices to Competitors." Their clubs were counted. The only thing missing was the rules official to accompany them.

Jim Bunch was assigned to that group, but he was nowhere in sight. Given all the rain delays at Bethpage State Park on Long Island, it was understandable. Bethpage was like JFK Airport in a snowstorm. Starting times were revised more often than a bill in Congress. Friday's second round finished on Saturday. I still do not know when this U.S. Open ended or, for that matter, if it did end. Oh, yes, it did. Lucas Glover eventually won.

Radio calls to Jim went unanswered. *What should I do now?* This was a first. I panicked.

A fellow was standing nearby, alone, inside the ropes. Nice-looking guy. He appeared official enough in an Open uniform. Little did he know. He was about to experience the walk of a lifetime.

"Are you an official?" I asked.

"Uh, yes," he said.

"Do you want to go with this group?"

"Sure," he said. He had an air of confidence.

But something told me to dig deeper.

"What's your name?" I asked.

"Dick Clark."

Dick Clark! Any teenager in the sixties knew that name. He was king of music and *American Bandstand* fame. "The world's oldest teenager."

"Do you want to dance?" It was the best I could muster at this anxious moment. He didn't think it was funny, and I returned to a more serious mode. Time was short.

"Where are you from?" I asked.

"New Jersey."

"Hmmm, New Jersey." I was now skeptical. "Hmmmm, you didn't attend the Committee dinner Wednesday night, did you?"

"No, I couldn't make it."

It was time. Jim Bunch was absent. Furyk, Casey, and Ogilvy were antsy. I made a hasty decision. Dick was hired.

He affirmed readiness. The players met their new referee. Little did we know that Dick Clark didn't have a *Rules of Golf* book.

Off they went. I relaxed, though still wondering about Jim Bunch. His absence was not like him. I worried.

For more than two hours, play continued on the rain-softened course. There was constant rules chatter on my radio. Thankfully, none of it was from Dick Clark.

With darkness approaching, an unusual radio call came my way. It was Jeff Hall, a USGA staff member who helps oversee the conduct of the U.S. Open in the areas of course setup and rules.

"Ron Read, did you send a referee with the Paul Casey group?"

"Ummm, yes, I think so." Hall did not seem comforted by my hesitancy. "Why are you asking?" I wondered.

"Paul Casey needs a ruling on No. 10," Hall said. "He has casual water. There's no referee."

Our rookie ref was gone, nowhere to be found. Was he in a comfort station or perhaps getting a bite to eat? AWOL was not acceptable.

Now, we had two missing officials! Another rules official was dispatched to assist Casey.

Suddenly, it was clear. This Dick Clark was not a certified rules official.

The snafu was not his fault. The starter shanked it, again.

With the assignment going smoothly, Dick disappeared. Years later, I learned he raced to more pressing duties as a volunteer in Scoring Central.

Dick Clark refereed only once—for eight holes—on golf's biggest stage. It was one-and-fun.

As for Jim, he just didn't get the word.

* * *

While enjoying lunch at the 2015 Open at Chambers Bay, I overheard a gentleman named Dick Clark being introduced to a large group at a table nearby. My antenna went up. Could it be?

I rushed to the table to meet this Dick Clark. Sure enough, it was the same guy. We shared a good laugh. On that fateful day six years earlier, he was very comfortable with the assignment I gave him. For over a decade, Dick was scoring supervisor at U.S. and British Opens. Today, he's an attorney in Austin, Texas, still volunteering for golf.

16

Being Put in
My Place—Again

WE CAN ALL LEARN PLENTY FROM OUR YOUTH. I certainly did. On this particular day, lucky young men were trying to qualify for the 2008 U.S. Junior Championship at the Los Angeles Country Club.

The second qualifying round was about to begin. Next on the first tee was a young golfer from San Diego. He and I were killing time in conversation.

A month earlier, Tiger Woods had won the U.S. Open at Torrey Pines, near the boy's home.

Seeing the name of his hometown, I conducted a little Q&A.

"Did you attend the Open?"

"Yes."

"Did you get to the first tee?"

"Yes, on Thursday morning." He was not a lad of many words.

"Oh, did you see Tiger's group with Phil (Mickelson) and Adam (Scott)?"

"Yes." His level of excitement rivaled a visit to the dentist.

"Did you see the starter?"

"Yes." He showed no sign of realizing my responsibility at Torrey Pines.

"Was the starter good?" I was clearly more excited than him.

"He was pretty good."

"*Pretty* good?" My voice rose.

"Yeah, pretty good."

"*What could he do better?*"

"When he said *some* names, he said them louder—like they were more important than others."

"Like *who*?!!" I was now nearly shouting.

"Well, when he introduced Tiger, he said, 'Tiger WOOOOODS!' He didn't do that for any other players."

"Oh, OK, I'll try to improve." I was properly humbled and somewhat deflated.

The young man made a good point and taught me. We are never too old to learn. I worked hard to never make that mistake again.

17

2008: Torrey Pines —
Tiger, Phil, and Adam

Febuary 9, 2008, was an important date in usga history. It was probably more meaningful to me than to others.

At 7:00 A.M., the world of golf learned that Chambers Bay would host the 2010 U.S. Amateur and the 2015 U.S. Open. I elaborate on that later.

Two minutes later, I called John Bodenhamer, then executive director of the Pacific Northwest Golf Association. We celebrated the news, and I suggested the Washington State Golf Association's home course be part of the scheme for the Amateur in 2010.

Later that Saturday, I was advised of a change in tradition at the U.S. Open in June at Torrey Pines.

For as long as anyone could remember, the pre-eminent starting time at the U.S. Open was the grouping of the Open champion, the U.S. Amateur champion, and the U.S. Open champion. But that was about to change.

Jon Miller, then the NBC president of programming, informed me of the change. Players one, two, and three in the world rankings would play together. That meant Tiger Woods, Phil Mickelson, and Adam Scott would comprise the featured grouping for the first two days.

Jon elaborated. At 8:06 A.M. in Round One of the Open, every NBC network around the world would go to Matt Lauer, co-host of *The Today Show*. After a lead-in,

Matt would say, "We go now to San Diego and to first-tee starter Ron Read at the U.S. Open at Torrey Pines."

Jon's closing words stayed with me.

"Don't screw it up!" he laughed.

Those words were again a reminder of Hannigan's 1986 send-off to me, "Welcome to show biz."

For the next five months, I practiced. Jon's chilling words were motivating.

The introduction of Scott received most of my attention. The previous year at Oakmont, I mistakenly said he was from Queensland, *England*, not Queensland, Australia, his native country. After that blunder, Adam just smiled and made no attempt to correct me. The heads-up from Jon gave me five months to block the gaffe from memory.

Then came the big day, Thursday at Torrey Pines.

At 8:05 A.M., I took several deep breaths and awaited a cue. A minute later, word came.

"Go!" Roger Maltbie instructed.

First to play was Scott. He had forgiven me for the miscue at Oakmont, though most of Australia had not. At this highly anticipated moment of high anxiety, Adam appeared uncomfortable, understandably nervous, and even out-of-place on golf's biggest stage in the company of Phil and Tiger.

The intro went perfectly. In apology to all Down Under, my voice emphasized Australia.

Adam's drive defied my amateur assessment of his state of mind. He was at ease. The ball went rapidly out of my sight on this bright sunny morning. It was a good one. In England, where's he's been a part-time resident, they would describe it as a "cracker."

Second was Mickelson, San Diego's hero. The crowd's shouting and applause drowned out the enunciation of his hometown, Rancho Santa Fe.

He brushed his visor, flashed a boyish smile, then gave them the drive they expected.

Two balls were safely in play.

Lastly, it was Tiger's turn to play. His drive went left—way left. Departing the tee, Tiger's slight limp was noted. His double-bogey start was no indication of the week to come.

I grinned, thinking, "Take that, Jon Miller."

The start had gone well. Jon would be happy.

There was no time to gloat after that pairing. The 8:17 grouping—Lee Janzen, Steve Flesch, and Rich Beem—was already present.

They wanted to see golf history, too. This was the first time the so-called "World Rankings" were being used in making pairings.

18

1983: Anger and Hilarity in the Skies

T HE SINGLE-ENGINE PLANE FLEW LOW OVER OAKMONT COUNTRY CLUB. The intrusion was in the final round of the 1983 U.S. Open. It pulled a banner that read, "Iron City Light Beer" Considering the hot, steamy weather, we all could have used some.

The plane's flight pattern was prohibited. The FAA supposedly was on alert. No planes were to enter the club's airspace. Oakmont was to be treated like the White House; only, it seems, one pilot did not get the word.

Harry Easterly was the head of the USGA staff. Harry was a graduate of Virginia Military Institute and had served in the Marine Corps in World War II. Sight of this unwanted aircraft seemed to reactivate Harry's military background.

"Get the plane's number on the wings," Harry ordered over the walkie-talkies that every official carried. Rules officials, scattered throughout the course, looked to obey the order and peered skyward.

"The first number is 6," one reported.

"The last number is 4," another radioed. No one was able to get a complete sighting, but eventually, the entire number was collected.

Almost two years earlier—August 5, 1981—President Reagan had fired all air traffic controllers.

Jim Farrell was one of those casualties. The FAA's loss was the USGA's gain. Jim joined the staff as a regional manager, the same position I held in the West. Jim called

Harry to report he still had old contacts at the FAA, and he could help identify the culprit.

In the meantime, the plane had disappeared for a time, then returned. This time, it had a new banner. If I remember correctly, the new banner read, "Giovanni's Pizza," a perfect complement to the beer banner it had pulled earlier.

Jim's effort was proving futile. It was not on the FAA's administrative radar, but there it was again in our sight.

This went on for about an hour. Then came a third banner. I think it was for "Spumoni." Beer and pizza and ice cream—a perfect trifecta.

None of this was sitting well with our boss. Everyone on the USGA's radio network sensed a nervous build-up.

Play continued. Larry Nelson, Tom Watson, Gil Morgan, and Seve Ballesteros battled away. The only thing they probably noticed was a buildup of dark clouds.

Adding to our problems away from play was the sighting of a fellow nicknamed "Rockin' Rollin." He frequented Tour events in those days, always managing to get into the front row of a gallery and in full sight of television cameras. His "rainbow" hairdo was decades ahead of its time. He was harmless, only wanting to show a religious sign—John 3:16.

Amid the chaos, Easterly dispatched me to "find him and remove him from the golf course."

Off I raced in hot pursuit of Rockin' Rollin. I stood on top of a golf cart, scanning the crowd, but I failed in the assignment. Like the plane, "Rockin'" was stealthy. He probably left the premises as thunderhead clouds grew more ominous.

At the same time, Harry Easterly had seen enough. The plane's third banner was all he could handle. Like General MacArthur, he gave a final order over the radio: "Get a plane and get him down!"

Obviously, no one knew exactly what this meant. It wasn't as though USGA had a plane and a pilot standing by for emergency action.

Anyone who heard the order probably remembers his precise location on hearing Harry's command. I had managed to climb off the top of that golf cart and had made my way to the locker room. On hearing the order, I collapsed in laughter on a locker bench.

What finally ended the hilarity?

Mother Nature did her thing. She sent a thunderstorm that sent everyone scattering for safety.

What became of the mysterious plane? We never knew where it landed. My hunch is its pilot was laughing and enjoying his banner's products.

19

1988: Strange Open in Beantown

ONE THING BECAME CLEAR UPON ARRIVING AT THE COUNTRY CLUB IN BROOKLINE, MASSACHUSETTS, IN 1988. This U.S. Open would be exciting, and it would not only be for the week of great golf.

As I walked into the landmark clubhouse, the boss, P. J. Boatwright Jr., spotted me, appearing lost. He suggested we have lunch. It was the Friday before Open week and a menu was not necessary. Boston clam chowder was required, but before our order got delivered to us, we were rousted from the genteel surroundings.

A voice from somewhere ordered us to evacuate the old, wooden clubhouse immediately! We were told a bomb could blow up any minute. It was not the quiet luncheon we expected. We ran, quite possibly for our lives.

Run, but to where? I had no idea where the nearest point of safety might be. Once outside, everybody scattered. I spotted a deep bunker near the clubhouse and dove into it. It was surreal. I hunkered, head down, covered only by my arm.

For me, it was a déja vu moment. My mind flashed back two decades.

I suddenly remembered back to when I was a private in the U.S. Army and was in basic training. An angry drill sergeant was teaching us to pull the pin on a grenade—a real grenade, then to throw it as fast and as far as we could. Then, he screamed, "Hit the ground!"

I took the threat at TCC as seriously as my 1967 grenade lesson at Fort Leonard Wood, Missouri.

It seemed an eternity in that sand bunker at the eighteenth green, but it was probably only ten or fifteen minutes. Eventually, we received an "all clear." Now gritty and sweaty, we returned to lunch. The clam chowder was cold, but it mattered not.

It had been quite a welcome to the U.S. Open.

This was my first visit to this historic club that was founded in 1882. TCC was one of five clubs that formed the USGA in 1894. This would be its third Open. The previous two ended in epic playoffs.

In 1913, amateur Francis Ouimet, at age twenty, defeated legendary British professionals Harry Vardon and Ted Ray. Ouimet, who lived across the street from TCC, was accompanied by ten-year-old caddie Eddie Lowery. Ouimet's playoff victory was the impetus for the sports film, *The Greatest Game Ever Played*, and his victory is arguably the biggest upset in golf history.

In 1963, Julius Boros defeated Arnold Palmer and Jacky Cupit in another eighteen-hole playoff at TCC.

Would 1988 be the club's third playoff?

For fifteen minutes, I wasn't sure it would even start.

No, this was not to be a quiet week, one focused only on the golf. After the bomb episode, I tiptoed around the clubhouse, fearing I might set off another alert—or worse.

Friday's ruckus was caused by a golf journalist, who had offended a political group in Northern Ireland. He commented on Irish drinking habits, saying they all acted like "drunken sailors."

My assignments that week were multiple. I oversaw Player Registration, then acted as liaison to the players, dealing with their needs. First, I greeted all 156 contestants and their families. That duty went quietly. Later, we took many players to Fenway Park to see Boston's beloved Red Sox play the New York Yankees. The only thing Boston hated more than the Yanks was its manager, Billy Martin. We saw proof of that one evening at dinner. Billy and his entourage arrived at our restaurant, heavily guarded.

As evidenced by the excitement at the U.S. Open, Billy and the Yankees weren't the only ones needing security.

On Wednesday morning, the USGA's Tony Zirpoli and Michael Butz toured the golf course—troubleshooting the day before Round One. It was also their last chance to see a bit of golf, albeit practice rounds before assignments put them largely behind the scenes and kept them there.

* * *

While I happened to be watching Seve Ballesteros and Greg Norman putt out somewhere on the front nine, another unusual thing happened. The two golfers were joined on the green by a spectator who had slipped under the gallery ropes. The guy wasn't seeking autographs or a photo. Instead, he began shouting, "Repent! Repent!"

It didn't bother the players or caddies. Seve and Greg kept putting. Talk about concentration!

The occurrence got the attention of Zirpoli and Butz, though. The staffers jumped from their golf cart and began running toward the intruder. Zirpoli had a radio. Breathing heavily as he raced to the green, Tony yelled into the radio, "Help! Help!" The alarm left everyone on the radio frequency wondering what was happening.

As Tony described it later, "The closer we got to the green, the bigger this guy got!"

None of this affected Ballesteros or Norman. They and their caddies watched as the USGA tag-team attempted to tackle the large man. Zirpoli and Butz each grabbed one of his legs, but they couldn't bring him down. The duo was losing badly.

As quickly as the intruder had appeared, so did a diminutive Boston policeman. The officer handcuffed the guy, using only one hand to do it. Seve and Greg putted through the entire melee.

Later, we learned the man had a history. He went by the name of John Charles Nicklaus III, claiming a relationship to Jack. His nickname was Kodiac Charlie.

After the incident, we learned later that the Nicklaus family, Ben Crenshaw, and Curtis Strange had restraining orders against him. If Kodiac ever got near them, he would be jailed. After this episode, he was locked up at Boston's Beth Israel Deaconess Hospital. The poor guy had a history of mental health disorders.

This was the end of the Kodiac story, or so we thought.

With the Open running more peacefully, Tony and I were backstage early Sunday afternoon. We were sitting near Frank Hannigan, who had moved on from the USGA to help explain the rules on ABC broadcasts of USGA championships. As Frank sat by patiently, Tony and I watched the broadcast on TV, nearby, quietly, so as not to bother Frank, who intently watched, too.

Suddenly, Zirpoli leaped to his feet.

"There he is!"

"Kodiac" was in Curtis Strange's gallery.

At the same time, Curtis spotted him in the gallery, too. This time, there was a group fracas and the gallery did what Zirpoli and Butz could not. Security appeared quickly, and the large pseudo-bear was again hauled away.

A short time after that episode, I got a radio call, asking me to assist ABC cameraman Don Langford, who went by the nickname of Peaches.

The crowds all week were enormous. Obviously, not everybody in Boston was watching the Red Sox-Yankees series. Peaches needed my help driving him and his heavy camera equipment through the crowds to vantage points. It was hot and steamy. We zigzagged through the throngs following the leaders. Late Sunday, I left the cart and bent over to lift a gallery rope in order to make way for our golf cart. To my surprise and embarrassment, there was a loud *rrrriiiippppp*.

It was my trousers! They were suddenly quite airy. Peaches thought this was funny. I didn't.

While I considered my plight, the bleacher crowds at the eighteenth were becoming unruly. It was really hot, and they were thirsty. They were also restless, waiting for slow golfers. One bleacher started chanting as though they were at Fenway Park. "Less filling!" they roared, and another grandstand responded in kind, "Tastes great!"

Back and forth they went, stereophonically. It was a verbal "wave."

The Country Club at Brookline was again making golf history. The National Open had never seen anything so raucous.

Peaches and I enjoyed the banter from a couple hundred yards away. Suddenly, he decided to capture this impromptu, historic moment.

"Let's go!" Peaches wanted me to escort him to the eighteenth green, where Miller Brewing was about to get free advertising courtesy of our cameraman.

Given my embarrassing situation, I disobeyed his order.

"You're on your own, pal." Carefully, this time, I lifted the gallery rope, allowing him to race under.

While Peaches sped to the action, I slinked my way to behind the eighteenth green, hoping to be unnoticed. Zirpoli joined me in the back row, where nobody could see my backside. Together, we guarded the Open trophy, secretly praying it would soon be presented. We watched in horror when Strange hit a three-wood followed by a seven-iron into the front bunker, the same one in which I had hunkered down during the bomb scare. I'm glad I had raked it nicely.

Only then did it dawn on Zirpoli and me. We could have a tie!

If Strange got the bunker shot up and down for par, we could put the trophy back in its case. If he was unnerved by Kodiac, Curtis did not show it. He blasted to three feet, then holed the putt to tie Nick Faldo at six under par. The Country Club would have its third eighteen-hole Open playoff.

With trousers mended by hand, I drove Peaches through the huge crowds on Monday.

Strange scored 71 to Faldo's 75. At the ceremony, I handed the Open trophy to USGA President William C. Battle for its presentation, one Virginian to another Commonwealth resident. Little did we know that the two Virginians would team again in 1989, when Strange became the first back-to-back U.S. Open champion since Ben Hogan in 1950 and 1951.

The U.S. Open will return to The Country Club in 2022. Like previous Opens, it promises to be uniquely memorable. However, it can't be as strange as 1988. No way.

20

1996: Time to Spare
at Oakland Hills — Not

T HE PLAYERS ALWAYS CAME FIRST. Fairness to them was of paramount importance. It didn't matter to me if the player was a four-time Open champion or a player who struggled through local and sectional qualifying. This was the U.S. Open, the most democratic championship in golf, and golf is a game built on fairness, sportsmanship, and individual character.

It was my belief that players who battled through two stages of qualifying deserved the same treatment as the stars of the worldwide tours who were fully exempt into the Open. Everyone was equal. There were no exceptions. That's how the U.S. Open was conducted.

The principle of fairness was sometimes tested, as it was in the final pairing in 1996 at Oakland Hills Country Club, outside Detroit, Michigan. The issue was beyond my control, and it required quick action to decide what was fair.

That Sunday, Steve Jones and Tom Lehman were in the final pairing.

NBC's Mark Rolfing would accompany them on course. Mark's first job was to cue me when to start. My $39 watch was still the official time, but NBC was now in charge. TV would decide when to start. Its coverage was live to a worldwide audience. The start now depended on NBC's schedule of commercials.

In fairness to the players, I asked Tom and Steve to be flexible. They understood the adjustment. I also asked Mark to keep me informed on the orders radioed to him by executive producer Tommy Roy. In turn, I kept the players informed. My goal was to have them ready to play when I received the word from Mark.

Everything seemed in sync. Or so I thought.

Mark whispered that we had two minutes. I alerted Tom and Steve. During this time of tension, I rehearsed the start in my mind, while Tom and Steve tried to relax before their start.

To my surprise, the order came to start. The alert of two minutes was more like thirty seconds. This was not the kind of "fast play" we asked of players.

Clearly, Tom and Steve weren't ready. Neither had a ball, a club, or a glove.

"Gentlemen, good luck!" I began, intending it to alert them.

They weren't happy, and the looks on their faces conveyed as much. They grumbled something inaudible. I gave them a hand signal, attempting to say, without speaking, "I understand your plight."

Given the awkward situation, live on TV, with no erasure for a mistake, I decided to drag out the introduction, giving the players more time.

"Ladies . . . and . . . gentlemen, this . . . is . . . the . . . final . . . pairing . . . in . . . the 96th . . . United . . . States . . . Open . . . Championship . . . conducted . . . by . . . " It probably sounded like an old 78 rpm record from the old days played at 33-and-a-third speed. I was only trying to be fair to Tom and Steve.

While I droned on, they got the message. Yes, they rushed. Happy for me, their drives found the fairway. Off the pals went in pursuit of a major title.

I breathed a sigh of relief. It had been another long day without a break on the first tee. After a late lunch, I headed to the back nine holes. It was my first on-course visit that week to finally see some golf. When I arrived at the seventeenth hole, I witnessed something special, an incident that distinguishes golf from other games.

Tom and Steve were tied on the seventy-first hole. Both had birdie putts on the par-3 seventeenth. Tom was aggressive on his birdie attempt, leaving him a treacherous and downhill three-footer for par. If he missed that one, the comeback putt would have been twice as long, and his chances would be over.

Tom marked his ball. Then, in the process of replacing the ball, the ball moved.

Tom froze and stopped. Only one person knew the ball had moved—its owner, Tom Lehman, and in those days, it was a penalty if he caused the ball to move. From nearby, I sensed what might have happened.

Tom's look said it all. "I've just lost the U.S. Open."

With the Open title at stake, he asked referee Trey Holland to join him.

Dr. Holland had treated thousands of patients, some facing death. The good doctor personally knew the look and feeling of panic. He once crash-landed his plane. What he saw in Tom shocked even him.

"I've never seen anyone turn so white," Trey said later.

The two chatted privately. I knew the subject. Tom was forthcoming with the facts. Dr. Holland listened, knowing the outcome could determine the champion. Trey concluded Tom had done nothing to cause the ball to move. There would be no penalty. Color returned to Tom's face.

Now recomposed, Tom sank the putt. Tom and Steve were tied going to the seventy-second hole.

Tom drove left into a fairway bunker. His shoulders slumped. He immediately knew he could not reach the green. He bogeyed, and Steve parred. Tom and Davis Love III finished second.

What happened a month later made me a believer in karma. Tom Lehman won the Open Championship and the Claret Jug at Royal Lytham. He became the first American to win at Lytham in seventy years. Bobby Jones had been the last, in 1926.

Bobby Jones lost the 1925 U.S. Open by one stroke. On that occasion, his ball, at one point in the tournament, had moved after he had addressed it. Like Tom, Bobby was the only one to see the ball's movement. Without hesitation, he called the one-stroke penalty on himself. Later, when asked about the incident, Jones humbly said, "You might as well praise me for not robbing banks."

Like Bobby Jones, with everything on the line, Tom did the right thing. He risked it all, preserving what's special about our game. Isn't that golf?

21

1986: Lanny Wadkins: Who's on First?

O N THE WEEKEND ROUNDS IN 1986 AT SHINNECOCK HILLS, WORD CAME FROM ABC'S TELEVISION COMPOUND TO THE FIRST TEE. Terry Jastrow decided that ABC would televise the last five starting times live, worldwide.

I would be cued. TV was in control. As I awaited their orders, Frank Hannigan's words from early that morning were recalled.

"Welcome to show biz." Those words came back often in my head over the next twenty-four years.

As I nervously anticipated ABC's order, I reviewed the names and hometowns on my pairing sheet. Players in the first group to be announced were Lanny Wadkins of Dallas, Texas, and Tommy Nakajima from Narita, Japan. I repeated "Narita" several times in my mind. Deep breaths followed. This was no time for any errors.

Then came the word from ABC, "Go."

A gulp followed, plus one more deep breath.

"From Dallas, Texas . . . Lanny Wadkins . . . "—there was applause. I had asked the gallery to clap, giving me time to regain my composure. "….and from Narita, Japan, Tommy Nakajima… "Mr. Nakajima has the honor. Play away, please."

Both looked at each other. They were puzzled.

Lanny was not supposed to have a speaking part, but nobody told him. He was always excellent at expressing feelings.

"I have the honor," he said, loud enough for the worldwide audience to hear.

What should I do now? That was my first thought.

Another gulp ensued. Lanny's comment was unexpected.

Lanny had looked at the names on the scoring standard carried by kids who accompanied the players. Lanny's name was on top of the standard, listed first. That was a mistake. Technically, I was right. Lanny was wrong.

My second thought was to picture Hannigan in the TV tower, asking himself, "Why did I give him that job?"

My third was to realize it was a no-harm, no-foul situation. Under the rules, in this circumstance, it did not matter who played first.

"Correction!" I said. "Mr. Wadkins has the honor. Play away, please."

From that moment, over the next twenty-five years, the word "correction" was always on the tip of my tongue. It remained there until the very end.

22

1994: Ernie Els at Oakmont

E RNIE ELS'S VICTORY WAS ANYTHING BUT EASY.
After a 66 on Saturday, he started the final round of the 1994 U.S. Open at Oakmont Country Club with a two-stroke lead over Frank Nobilo and a three-stroke advantage on Colin Montgomerie, Loren Roberts, and Tom Watson. Those margins appeared to be in immediate jeopardy.

Paired with Nobilo for the final round, Ernie yanked a drive left—far left—on No. 1. It is difficult to lose a ball at the Open, given the size of the crowds, but this ball was a candidate. He should probably have hit a provisional ball.

Referee Trey Holland and USGA President Reg Murphy raced to join Els's search. My assignment was to accompany them (once the last group had left the first tee), but first, I had to tidy things on the first tee.

With Nobilo safely in the fairway, Els's ball was located in a dire position. His lie might have been deemed unplayable by mortals. Even Ernie could, probably, only hack the ball back into the fairway. Complicating matters, he was behind a large TV truck. He wisely asked Holland for free relief from the truck directly on his line, and he was permitted to drop without penalty away from the intervening truck.

It wasn't until later that Dr. Holland realized the truck should have been moved if its driver could be found.

By receiving a drop, Els received a big break. It was not his last.

I scurried to the scene but was too late. I knew nothing about the ruling.

However, the gallery did, and several spectators were riled. Seeing the USGA logo on my shirt, a few expressed their displeasure in words not suitable for family conversation.

Listening to the abuse, I thought, "What happened here?"

Ernie scored 73, compared with 70 for both Montgomerie and Roberts. The three were tied. They would play eighteen more holes on Monday.

On the playoff's second hole, Els misclubbed, and his ball flew over the green and into dense bushes. I suspected its location and, alone, crawled on hands and knees into the suspected area.

I managed to find the ball, but by the time I crawled out, I was dirty, head to foot, with branches sticking to me. There was no place to change clothing or to hide, but Ernie had his ball. Now, what was he going to do with it?

After declaring the ball unplayable, he dropped behind the bushes on the third tee. He ended up with a triple-bogey 7. The title appeared out of Ernie's reach, but he battled back. He and Roberts tied with 74. When the playoff continued in a sudden-death format, Els parred No. 2 this time to claim his first U.S. Open title.

Did finding Ernie's ball affect the outcome? It is doubtful. He might have scored lower had I not found his ball. I was the only one to go into the shrubs, and I emerged looking like a porcupine. Also, Ernie could have simply stopped any search by declaring the ball lost. I know this much: If he had declared it lost to start with, I would have appeared much cleaner and not looked like a porcupine.

23

1992: Pebble Beach — Tom Smith: 'I Need a Driver, Stat!'

"WHAT WAS THE MOST INTERESTING REQUEST EVER MADE OF YOU WHILE ON THE FIRST TEE?"

If I were to be asked that, I would have two answers.

One was that from Payne Stewart before his final round in 1999 at Pinehurst. He wanted a pair of scissors. (I'll get back to that later in the book.)

The second unusual request came from pro Tom Smith before the first round in 1992 at Pebble Beach.

"Where can I get a driver?" Smith asked.

There was proverbial "steam" coming from Tom's ears. I didn't yet know what had riled him, but I was about to find out.

"Where's your caddie?" I asked.

"I don't know," he groused. "I need a driver."

"Go to the golf shop and ask to borrow a driver," I ordered.

He had less than three minutes until his start. Smith ran thirty yards to the pro shop. He quickly returned—without a club.

"They don't have one," he barked.

"Go back in there and see Sally Dodge, and hurry!"

I knew Sally could solve anything. Now Smith had less than two minutes.

With less than thirty seconds to go, he was back, huffing and mad, but he had a driver from a rental set of clubs. His caddie was still missing.

"From Selma, Alabama . . . Tom Smith. Play away, please," I said.

"This will be interesting," I thought.

Smith had never hit a ball with this club. The driver was from a well-used rental set, and the shaft was "soft" and whippy, meant for golfers three times Tom's age. I watched the drive with added interest. Given his state of mind, the ball might go anywhere.

Somehow, Smith's ball found the center of the fairway. Most players hit long irons or short metal clubs on No. 1 at Pebble Beach. This drive was aided by the redness shown on his face and probably elsewhere.

He stomped back to stand by my side as others played.

Suddenly, his caddie joined us. Tom's grimace spoke volumes. So did the toss he gave the borrowed club to the ground.

What followed was amazing. It was a one-way conversation. Tom spoke, but his lips didn't move. He reminded me of ventriloquist Edgar Bergen, who made us all laugh with dummies Charley McCarthy and Mortimer Snerd. This was, however, no laughing matter. Tom's vocabulary was replete with every bad word Mom told me never to say. I was the only one to hear Tom's monologue lecture.

"I won't see this partnership tomorrow." I was certain.

Off they went on what promised to be an interesting day of golf and demeanor.

If Tom Smith had a sports psychologist (as most golfers do, as part of their 'team'), that person apparently did a remarkable job overnight.

Tom and his caddie arrived together the next day. There was no sign of Thursday's brouhaha.

Sunday, Tom Kite was crowned champion.

A day later, I reflected on the week, my third Open at Pebble Beach. Only then did I realize another of my gaffes.

For one brief moment, Tom Smith had fifteen clubs, one more than allowed in Rule 4. The penalty is two strokes.

Imagine how Smith, with his body temperature already at 212 degrees, would have reacted if the starter had said, "Tom, please add two more strokes to your score."

24

1983: Forrest Fezler—A Shorts Story

"WHY ME?" IT WAS ANOTHER ONE OF THOSE MOMENTS.

Forrest Fezler approached me in the locker room before the final round at Oakmont in 1983. He asked a question that puzzled me. It was a new one.

"What will you (USGA) do if I wear Bermuda shorts?" he asked.

"I have no objection," I said. "If Oakmont allows shorts, it's fine with me, but let me check."

I sought counsel from Frank Hannigan. The answer he gave proved valuable countless times over the next thirty years.

There was more to Forrest's request than I was aware, and Frank shared the rest of the story.

Frank told me that earlier that week, P. J. Boatwright Jr. spotted Forrest during a practice round and had to look several times before he believed his eyes. The colorful dresser was wearing shorts. Such attire was a violation of the dress code on the PGA Tour, but all the players know that the U.S. Open is not a Tour event. Forrest knew that, too, and he wisely asked what the USGA's policy would be.

P. J. met with Forrest and they resolved the matter of on-course attire. Forrest could finish the practice round in shorts, but he would not wear them again. The Tour's dress code would be upheld.

Knowing there was "history" between Forrest and P. J., the resolution seemed magnanimous on the rules icon's part.

The history went back two years, to the 1981 U.S. Open at Merion.

P. J. had penalized Forrest and John Schroeder for slow play when they finished twenty minutes behind the group ahead of them, but the committee later overturned the decision. The reversal settled well with some, but most players shook their heads in support of P. J.'s initial ruling. Players know the culprits, and Forrest and Schroeder were well known as deliberate. The reversal was never personal to P. J., and it had no impact on P. J.'s decision at Oakmont. All was forgiven.

That Sunday at Oakmont, Frank suggested I remind Forrest of his agreement with P. J., and he left me with some strong words.

"Tell him to let his conscience be his guide."

Off I went to find Forrest. I caught him in the locker room before the final round.

Forrest now added to his dilemma. The maker of those Bermuda shorts would pay him $3,500, as I recall, if he wore shorts.

I listened. My final words to Forrest were the parting words Hannigan wanted conveyed: "Let your conscience be your guide." Keep in mind, there's nothing in the *Rules of Golf* to prohibit a player from wearing shorts—to include in a U.S. Open— and the only thing Fezler would be violating if he were to wear shorts would be P. J.'s stated opinion about such apparel.

The final decision was being left to Forrest Fezler. I thought that would end the matter. I was wrong.

After playing his seventy-first hole, Forrest slipped into a portable restroom and came out wearing shorts. The crowd on eighteen loved it.

Remember, Forrest's caper did not violate the *Rules of Golf,* although some golf purists might have viewed it differently.

Hannigan's words became valuable many times in applying the rules in other situations, such as a player's disagreement with an opinion given by an official. In those one-on-one situations, with facts clear, I often allowed the player to decide his own fate.

"Here's what I believe you did," I once told a lad. "And, here's the rule. Apply the rule. Let your conscience be your guide. You'll sleep better tonight."

He did. Isn't that what makes golf different?

25

Bernhard Langer Beats the Clock

BERNHARD LANGER DREW ATTENTION FOR HIS PUTTING STYLE. When "anchored putting" (whereby a player anchors one of his hands against his body while in his stance and keeps it there during his subsequent putting motion) was banned by golf's governing bodies, he modified his stroke slightly. Some argued he still anchored. In response, he claimed his hands were not touching his body and, thus, not anchored.

Authorities sided with Bernhard's explanation.

Others howled.

I didn't. I believed him.

One thing is clear. The most accomplished German golfer ever has been successful around the world for more than thirty years.

Bernhard's unique putting stroke was not his first brush with controversy. He has never been known as a fast player. His deliberate play gained the attention of rules officials over many years.

I was a rules official for more than forty years. Pace of play, or slow play, has been an issue from Day One. During that time, many procedures have been attempted to speed up play. Each "pace system" required timing of players only after they were out of position. Each system had one problem. The problem in monitoring was in determining when an official precisely started the clock.

If twenty officials were asked to time players, there would probably be twenty different times on how long the player took. Each would be based on when the official started his clock.

Bernhard is not only a great golfer, he's also a bright and honorable gentleman. He recognized the dilemma for officials.

It seemed Bernhard knew how to beat the clock.

I started Bernhard from the first tee in nineteen U.S. Opens. Over that time, he often teed the ball once, then picked it up and re-teed it in another location. There were times when he teed a third time. Nobody did it more.

Bernhard made it difficult for anyone to know exactly when to start the clock.

After watching his quirky habit, I often had some fun.

Before introducing him, I asked the walking official for a small wager.

"I'll bet you a buck he re-tees the ball," I posed.

My winnings over the years could buy a round at Oktoberfest. I seldom lost and never collected.

Under the new rules that became effective in 2019, forty seconds is the suggested time for any stroke.

Want to bet if it will be enforced?

26

1992: Where's Oswestry?

I T ALL BEGAN HARMLESSLY ENOUGH.

"Ladies and gentlemen, this is the final pairing in the 92nd United States Open Championship, conducted by the United States Golf Association."

"The players are . . . Ian Woosnam of Oswestry, England . . . "

"I'm from Wales," Ian suddenly blurted.

The interruption flustered me. This was being aired worldwide, live, and I had no erasure.

"Correction," I said, "Wales."

For the first three rounds, Woosnam had passively accepted his introduction from Oswestry, England, without comment. That is precisely where he told me he lived.

I collected my composure and introduced Gil Morgan, the leader, correctly, from Edmond, Oklahoma.

Next, the officials were introduced.

"The referee is Stuart Bloch, president of the USGA. Mr. Bloch is from Wheeling, West Virginia.

"The observer is Reg Murphy, vice president of the USGA. Mr. Murphy is from Baltimore, Maryland."

Still unnerved by the Woosnam correction, the really big whopper was about to roll off my lips.

"The special observer is Mr. Joe Carr, Captain of the Royal and Ancient Golf Club, of St. Andrews, Scotland. Mr. Carr is from Dublin, *England*."

There was a buzz around me. Something was wrong. I stopped and looked in Joe's direction. He was smiling broadly. My mistake became apparent.

"Correction," I said for a second time. "Dublin, *Ireland*."

Next to speak from the ABC booth was Englishman Peter Alliss, a man with a lightning fast wit, working for both ABC and BBC. He had a grasp of the political incorrectness of my gaffe, and the error did not miss Peter's attention.

"Wars . . . have started over less," he boomed around the globe.

Several hours later, I cornered David Fay at the "Toast to the Champion" party.

"David, I never asked for this job." I said. "You can have it."

He attempted to mollify me. A glass of merlot did a somewhat better job than he could.

Two days later, I was still feeling the effects of my embarrassing mistake.

I was at a restaurant in San Ramon, California, alone. The waiter asked my drink order. It was another merlot. From his accent, I sensed his nationality.

"Where are you from?" I asked.

"England . . . London, actually," he said.

"Do you know where Oswestry is?"

"Yes. It borders Wales," he related. Then, his whopper. "Uh, I was watching the U.S. Open . . . "

I felt sick again.

"Oh, no!" I said. In an instant, a migraine returned. My head was in my hands, already throbbing while trying to forget. I sensed what was coming.

"You're the guy!" he exclaimed. His voice could be heard throughout the restaurant. He somehow recognized me as the bloke who had made the intro blunder.

Without another word, he turned and raced to the bar.

"He's the guy," he said to the bartender.

His reaction was the perfect antidote. At that moment, I realized the hilarity of the situation. My mistake had hurt no one.

Little did I know the distance this incident would travel. Seven years later, my son, Ryan, and I had played golf in Macrihanish, Scotland. A group from Dublin's Portmarnoch Golf Club was seated next to us. Portmarnoch was Joe Carr's club. The story of the 1992 Open intro came out.

"You're famous at our club!" they said.

Again, we laughed. Since that dinner in San Ramon, I haven't stopped.

27

2003: The Flag:
Back Where It Belongs

I T STARTED WITH A ROAR IN 1982. Twenty-one years later, it ended in a bit of an up-roar.

In the beginning, Tom Watson faced a delicate pitch shot at the seventy-first hole of the 82nd U.S. Open at Pebble Beach. At that exact moment, Jack Nicklaus was being interviewed by ABC's Jack Whitaker at the eighteenth green. Happiness showed in the faces of the pair of Jacks. Whitaker's question was something like, "Jack, how does it feel to win your fifth U.S. Open?"

Before Nicklaus could respond, thunderous applause came from the seventeenth green. Its message was clear. Watson had made birdie.

Some six hundred yards away, USGA's Tom Meeks was watching a TV monitor in the scoring tent near the interview. He confirmed what we already knew. Nicklaus's face turned white. His fifth U.S. Open title would have to wait, and the interview took a much different tone. Barring a collapse on the seventy-second hole, Tom Watson would win, and golf's "shot heard 'round the world" would be remembered forever.

Twenty-one years later—Father's Day 2003—began like most for me, in darkness. That was not new. Most championship days did. I was scrounging through a suitcase trying not to wake my wife, Missy. I was searching for two things.

One was the Socks. These were not just any socks; these were special. I had worn them on the first tee on every Father's Day since 1989, at Oak Hill, where I had first opened them out of a package for me. They were a gift from our children—Alicia and Ryan. They were truly now holey in a literal sense. More importantly, the wording on each was, "I Love Dad."

At the same time in 1989, Jack Nicklaus was next to me, opening a card from his daughter, Nan. Simultaneously, there were two grown men on the first tee at the U.S. Open, each shedding tears, emotionally struck by our children. Championship golf was taking a back seat. Only our kids mattered in that moment, twenty-one years earlier, in 1989.

The second thing I sought in darkness from the suitcase was special, too. It was a flag. This one had historical golf significance. It was from the seventeenth hole at Pebble Beach, where Tom Watson had pitched into the hole to eventually win the 1982 U.S. Open.

The flag had been sitting, folded, in a box for twenty-one years. Frankly, I had forgotten about it. I brought it to Olympia Fields, hoping Tom might sign it. Neither of us was getting younger, and Tom had announced this would be his last Open. This could be my last chance.

Wearing "I Love Dad" socks and carrying the prized flag, I arrived at Olympia Fields at sunrise. After organizing the first tee for an 8:00 A.M. start, I returned to the locker room, hoping to find Tom and to have him sign it.

As I wandered the maze of the gigantic locker room, looking for Watson, an interesting thing happened. It was unrelated to my search for Tom. I ran into two Chicago policemen in their distinctive checkered hats. They were accompanied by a friend, the largest German Shephard dog I had ever seen. After a brief chat, I asked about the dog. It was discomforting to learn the dog was looking for bombs.

"What does Rin Tin Tin do when he finds a bomb?" I asked timidly.

The officer did not respond. Instead, he removed a bag from his pocket. The bag contained a white powder. He tossed the bag onto a very tall bar.

"Rinny" stopped eyeing me, thankfully. The bag now had his attention. It didn't contain a rib roast. Instead, it was dynamite! He leaped high over a bar stool and onto the bar. After this demo, I was comforted at what was going on behind the scenes to keep us safe.

My search for Watson continued, though I was now multitasking. While I still sought Tom, I was also assisting Rinny, peering everywhere for suspicious packages. Happily, I never found one. I did not find Watson, either. It gave me time to develop a better idea.

Watson had become the biggest story at the Open. His opening 65 was the lowest round by anyone.

However, there was a sad sidebar story to this, too. Bruce Edwards, Tom's long-time caddie, was suffering from ALS. The incurable disease was dormie 3 over Edwards. He had three years to live—maybe. The result of his match with ALS was already posted. Fatal.

Unable to find Tom, I decided that Bruce should own the flag. I did not clear that decision with Bruce's boss or with anyone at the USGA. It seemed a private matter and the right thing to do.

Sunday afternoon, Bruce came up the hill to the first tee, lugging Tom's heavy bag. He was solo. Tom was nowhere in sight. The challenge of the disease Edwards faced was showing.

Without explanation, I presented Bruce the flag.

"What's this?" Bruce asked.

"It's the flag from the seventeenth hole in 1982," I explained.

He appeared skeptical.

"Bruce, I've had the flag all these years," I said. "I got it from the USGA office on the Monday after."

He became teary-eyed. So did I. There was silence. It was as quiet as that moment before Watson's putt to win the 1982 Open.

Tom suddenly appeared. He looked at the emotional scene. I think he said, "What's going on here?"

Bruce showed Tom the flag, then moved toward the tee to get ready for play.

"I tried to find you this morning," I confessed. "I wanted to have you sign it. Then, I thought about Bruce. Did I do the right thing?" It became emotional again, now including Tom.

"You did the right thing," he said.

Moments later, it was game time. I recovered.

"Ladies and gentlemen, this is the 1982 United States Open champion, from Kansas City, Kansas . . . Tom Watson." It would have been nice to introduce Bruce, too.

An hour later, my duties at the first tee had ended. Marty Parkes, communications director for the USGA, called. He asked me to come to the media center to explain what had happened regarding Watson and Edwards before their start. It puzzled me that anyone else knew. Writers were asking.

"Marty, it was a private matter," I said. "No big deal." I declined my friend's request.

At about 3:00, as Missy and I were having a late lunch, we got a surprise. We heard NBC's Jimmy Roberts do what he does best. He told the story about the flag. I shook my head in disbelief. How did he know? Spies were everywhere, even at our Open.

The flag, I later learned, was auctioned the next day at a fundraiser for the Bruce Edwards Foundation in Kansas City. The best part is that Tom Watson got the flag. He still has it.

28

1999: Pinehurst: Amazing Grace

PAYNE STEWART WAS THE ONLY GUY, IN MY VIEW, WHO COULD LOOK TIGER WOODS, IN HIS PRIME, IN THE EYE AND SAY, "I CAN BEAT YOUR (BOTTOM)."

Payne's actual words would have been stronger than that. He exuded confidence on and off the golf course.

At the 1999 U.S. Open at Pinehurst No. 2, Payne had that look of confidence when he arrived on the first tee on Sunday at 2:54 P.M. He was six minutes early. That was uncommon. Something was up.

He was chomping on gum, as usual. His question surprised me.

"Do you have any scissors?" he asked.

Was he kidding? I treated his request lightly. Scissors were not a tool in the starter's kit.

I circled around him, up close.

"You don't need a haircut." By his look, I knew he was serious.

"No, I don't," he said. "I want to cut these sleeves."

It was drizzling lightly, and Payne was wearing an expensive rain suit. Everything he ever wore looked expensive. He once drove my son and me to our hotel; he was wearing gold-tipped golf shoes.

It was five minutes before he and Phil Mickelson would start their final rounds. Quick action was required.

I directed his caddie, Mike Hicks, to the tennis center about a block away.

"Run!" I said. I radioed ahead to alert the center.

Two minutes later, Mike returned with scissors! Without taking the jacket off, they made incisions. Payne was already a fashion plate in his plus-fours and Hogan cap. The sleeveless jacket with its fresh cuts was a new look in shabby elegance.

Payne's sleeveless jacket may have been the first in golf. The guy was always a trendsetter in golf fashion.

Mickelson was watching with a puzzled look. He had other important things on his mind, like the pending birth of his first child.

With the rain jacket newly tailored, the moment of high tension had arrived. Nobody spoke—inside the ropes or outside. The only sound was the light drizzle hitting the starter's tent. NBC's Mark Rolfing listened intently on his headset for orders to start player introductions. I awaited Mark's cue.

"Go!" Rolfing suddenly said.

As though on command from above, the chimes at the nearby Village Chapel began playing a beautiful song, "Amazing Grace." Its sound cut both the silence and the tension.

I made a quick decision. This hymn superseded golf, even the National Championship, if only for the moment. NBC and the world could wait. We paused, briefly, until the hymn ended. It was a relaxing moment, one of tranquility perhaps never experienced in any previous U.S. Open.

Now, it was my turn.

"Ladies and gentlemen, this is the final pairing in the 99th United States Open Championship. From Scottsdale, Arizona . . . Phil . . . Mickelson. Play away, please."

Next, the leader.

"And, from Orlando, Florida, the 1991 United States Open champion . . . Payne . . . Stewart."

Only one knew what history would unfold, that day and in the future. He may have sent the song.

29

2004: Joe Ogilvie:
The Man Can Multitask

CONTROVERSY AT THE OPEN WAS NOTHING NEW. IT'S NEVER MORE THAN A GIMME PUTT AWAY.

The 1972 U.S. Open at Pebble Beach had been my first Open. Greens became so off-color and dry that year, they were called browns. By Sunday, many greens were said to be dead.

The 1974 U.S. Open was dubbed The Massacre at Winged Foot. Hale Irwin survived as winner at seven over par. Frank "Sandy" Tatum, who helped in the conduct of the U.S. Open for decades and served as president of the association, defended the result, famously saying, "We're not trying to embarrass the best players in the world. We're trying to identify them."

Players rebelled.

In 1976 at Atlanta Athletic Club, the USGA forgot to mow fairways before the first round. Players howled. The blunder didn't bother Irwin, whose 69 led amateur Bobby Clampett by one stroke.

In 1983, the USGA did something blasphemous to Oakmont's members. It cut the rough, after which chairman Richard Fuhrer gave USGA a proverbial "haircut." Maybe worse, it was rumored USGA slowed the greens from member play!

At Olympic in 1998, players were embarrassed by a risky hole location on the eighteenth green. Payne Stewart putted a ball from the side of the hole, then watched in disbelief as his ball missed the hole but didn't come to a stop. It began to trickle down toward the front of the green, rolling ever so slowly and leaving Stewart with 10 feet . . . then 12 . . . then 15 . . . then 20. Players and media skewered the USGA.

Tom Meeks, the USGA staff person in charge of course set-up, admitted an error.

And in 2015, the greens at Chambers Bay made turf experts out of everybody—players, media, and golf fans. This F-word, fescue, made headlines. The wonderful fescue grass in May lost a battle with Nature, and the heartier *poa annua* grass dominated in June, making greens less than ideally smooth. Despite the outcry, Jordan Spieth and Dustin Johnson finished one-two in a dramatic finish.

* * *

Then came Shinnecock Hills in 2004. This U.S. Open had become particularly contentious. There were complaints about the conditions at Shinnecock Hills, particularly the increasing dryness and firmness of the greens as the week went on. Mother Nature stirred the controversy. On Saturday night, high winds swept over the course. They subsided only slightly on Sunday. The course was firm, fast, and difficult. Some thought too hard. Retief Goosen did not. He might have played the finest Open round in history, scoring a one-over 71, given brutally difficult and windy conditions in a final round.

The center of malcontent was the seventh green. Though the hole played only 189 yards in that Open, the green angles away from play, making the target area even smaller, coupled with a green that tilts. Under the best of conditions, it's hard to keep a ball on the green. The design concept is called a *Redan*. Under Open conditions with gale winds, few could solve the problem.

The squabble had become very public. Players complained, which was not new. Media loved the criticism. Perhaps most importantly, the proud members of Shinnecock Hills grumbled, too. Their relationship with the USGA had deteriorated from 1986, when the USGA took the Open there for the first time in ninety years.

How bad were things? When I expressed to a club member that I looked forward to working with him at a future Open at Shinnecock, he said, "There won't be a next time!"

Ouch.

The relationship between the club and the USGA was prickly. Members were rankled by remarks made on the TV broadcast about course conditions. They defended superintendent Mark Michaud, who was overseeing his second Open, his first having been at Pebble Beach.

When Joe Ogilvie arrived for his 10:30 starting time, along with Jim Furyk, in the fourth round, he wanted to talk to me. Our conversation turned out differently than any other in my years on the first tee.

We exchanged Father's Day greetings. His mood was good, though he and Jim were fourteen strokes off Retief's lead. Then, Joe got to the point.

He had overheard disgruntled members in the locker room. Feelings at Shinnecock had become so raw that some members suggested suing the USGA. On what grounds? Nature's bias against entitled golfers?

The seriousness of Joe's revelation shocked me. After he left the tee, I phoned David Fay, the USGA executive director, to sound the alarm. David showed little concern. That was his nature—once again, reasoned and deliberate.

History proved David right. No lawsuit was filed. Reason prevailed. All was forgiven. The Open returned in 2018 to Shinnecock, although, unfortunately, there was more complaining. It was over a very few greens and a couple regrettable hole locations made even harder by windy conditions in Saturday's round.

Shinnecock Hills deserves better.

How good is Shinnecock Hills?

The late P. J. Boatwright Jr. oversaw the U.S. Open for more than two decades. Over several Dewar's and water, he confided a love of Shinnecock and Pebble Beach, A back-and-forth rotation of Shinnecock-Pebble Beach-Shinnecock-Pebble Beach with others occasionally sprinkled in would have suited him. He liked the generally moderate weather at Shinnecock and Pebble Beach that increased the likelihood of a four-day event without delays. TV liked that, too.

Before Joe left the tee, there was a light moment, which I needed. The bickering and talk of a lawsuit was unsettling.

At 10:30, conversation was ended. It was time for serious golf.

"From Austin, Texas, Joe . . . Ogilvie."

Joe suddenly became all business. The Duke grad's total focus came quickly. He selected a three-wood, took his stance, and addressed the ball. The silence became that of a church on Sunday.

Unexpectedly, a loud roar came from somewhere out on the course. Whatever had happened greatly excited the crowd. Something really good had happened. In the old days, it was the sound of a Nicklaus or Palmer birdie.

Joe stopped, unfazed. He looked up and smiled.

"Somebody just knocked it in on number seven," he said.

Ogilvie guessed wrong; it wasn't an ace. Maybe some of his fellow players were just excited this weekend was coming to a close.

30

The USGA Goes Green

WHO WOULD HAVE THOUGHT GOLF TEES COULD CREATE SUCH A BROUHAHA? These did.

It was sometime in the early 1990s. The tees were so bad they got a mulligan year.

With the world going "green," someone at the USGA decided our Open should, too. They ordered thousands of biodegradable golf tees.

The concept was sound. The tees were made with nutrients good for grass, and the broken pieces were easier on mowers. Sounds great, right?

I was instructed to put them in a bowl on the first tee. Players and caddies wondered how they would work but stuffed their pockets anyway. Everyone thought we were doing something positive for the environment.

That might have been true. But we were also doing good things for the dry-cleaning industry.

The biodegradable tees did something unanticipated. In humid and rainy weather, they degraded not only on tees, but also in players' and caddies' pockets.

Players did not make as big a fuss as the caddies did. Most players had clothing deals with manufacturers who filled their lockers and closets with the latest styles in shirts and slacks. They could easily afford to replace clothes.

Caddies were not so lucky. The caddie area had the sights and sounds of a prison riot. Shirts and slacks became color-stained, and green was no longer their favorite color.

Rumor was that the caddie of one prominent golfer might have threatened legal action against the well-meaning USGA. In the end, I believe the Open took a financial hit at the local laundry.

In cleaning out our offices after the Open, we found an unopened box. Inside, we found several thousand more tees. In the heat and humidity, they, too, had melted, forming one solid, biodegradable mass.

Here's hoping those tees found a resting place where they did more good than at the U.S. Open.

31

Arnie: Always Giving Fans What They Came to See

W HAT'S THE GREATEST FIRST-TEE SHOT OF ALL TIME? Some say Arnold Palmer's drive at Cherry Hills Country Club in 1960.

Trailing by seven shots, he lashed a persimmon wood. From some 346 yards away, the balata ball avoided a lateral hazard to the right, landed in the rough, and rolled onto the green. A two-putt birdie started his run back into contention. It led to a 65 and a three-stroke victory, his only U.S. Open title.

My candidate, however, was Arnold's drive thirty-three years later, in the 1993 U.S. Senior Open, when he was well into his sixties. It came at the same location, Cherry Hills. It was his first competitive round there since 1960.

Arnold surprised me that day. He arrived twenty minutes before his starting time. Players never arrived that early. They practiced on the range, or they stayed on the practice green until the players in the group in front of them headed to the first fairway. Palmer's premature arrival was unprecedented.

He joined me in the starter's tent. He did not wish to detract from others. As each player hit, Arnold popped his head out of the tent, paying close attention. Some played safely with irons or three-woods. A few hit drivers. He intently watched the six players in the two starting times preceding his. I finally figured out why.

He had a plan.

Arnold was turning back the clock. He was going to try to drive the green. Fans had not come to see him play safely. He knew that.

"Ladies and gentlemen . . . from Latrobe, Pennsylvania . . . Arnold . . . Palmer."

In the mile-high air, the applause may have been heard in downtown Denver, eight miles to the north.

He gave his trousers a patented tug. From watching others, he knew the wind was in his face. Also, he had to know it was unlikely he could reach the green, but he had made up his mind. He wasted no time pulling the metal-headed driver out of his bag. There was a message to his decisiveness: "I'm not going to play like a senior. I'm not playing safe!"

Those were Arnold's words at the 1982 Senior Open, when caddie David Jacobsen suggested a more conservative shot from the trees. In his own way, he was saying that again.

He gave his pants one more tug.

Knowing his plan, I peeked out of my tent. So did rules official Gerry Stahl. Could the Man do it again?

He gave the ball the same effort as in 1960. The ball took the similar path of thirty-three years earlier. It challenged the creek on the right, and it landed safely about fifty yards from the green, then began to bounce. The ball did not quite make it, settling within range of a sand wedge.

The outcome mattered not. The King had given thousands everything they had come to see.

32

Ready, Willing, and Able

THIS WAS ONE OF THE BEST SIGHTS EVER FROM THE FIRST TEE AT THE U.S. OPEN IN 2000 AT PEBBLE BEACH.

My son, Ryan, was climbing the grandstand steps behind the tee at Pebble Beach. I spotted him and waved.

The next introduction was Bernhard Langer. It had better be perfect or "Old Dad" would hear about it for a long, long time.

As Ryan sat down, Langer arrived. He was alone. His caddie was nowhere in sight.

Bernhard then surprised me.

"What's the deal with caddies?" he asked.

"Uh, what do you mean?"

"I need a caddie," he said. "I've sent mine to get a putter."

"Well, under the rules," I explained, "you can have one caddie at one time,"

As starter, it was not often that I had to cite the *Rules of Golf.*

"Well, I need a caddie," Bernhard said. He had clubs but nobody to carry them.

My mind raced. It was too late to radio for a caddie. A solution came to me. What about Ryan? Would Bernhard want him?

Time was short. A job interview was not possible. I began a selling job on the employer.

"Bernhard, my son has caddied at Pebble Beach," I said. "He knows the golf

93

course, and he knows the game. He's caddied in the Open at Congressional and the Mid-Am in Fresno. He won't embarrass you."

"Get him!" said the man in need.

"Ryan!" I bellowed. I had no idea whether he would take the assignment. He had barely had time to be seated. "Please come, and hurry!"

With a smile, he bounded down the steps from the grandstand. He had no clue what was about to happen.

Now, I had to do a selling job on Ryan.

"Ryan, Mr. Langer needs you to caddie," I said. "Will you do it? It may be one hole or several, just until his regular caddie arrives."

"Dad, are you kidding me?" Ryan said. I assured him we were serious. He accepted the job. There was no time to discuss salary. We had less than two minutes until Bernhard's start.

Ryan looked up at his bewildered friend sitting at the top of the grandstand, and another fifteen hundred fans in the bleacher wondered, too, what was happening.

"I'll see you later," he yelled to his friend.

There was no time to properly dress him in a caddie bib. He hoisted Langer's heavy golf bag and appeared ready to go.

"Ladies and gentlemen, please welcome from Anhausen, Germany . . . Bernhard . . . Langer. Play away, please."

His three-iron split the fairway.

There was applause. Maybe some of it was for the guest caddie. Or maybe not. Many were still wondering what had happened. Off they went.

When they arrived at his ball, Bernhard turned to Ryan and asked the distance.

"138." Like a good caddie, Ryan had already grounded the bag and had paced the distance from a sprinkler once familiar to him. It had been eight years since he had caddied at Pebble Beach.

"Hmmm, I got 126," the German said in perfect English. A difference of 12 yards was huge to a professional golfer.

They were speaking the same language but were already having a communication problem.

"Is that meters or yards?" Bernhard asked.

"Yards," Ryan said.

The two-time Masters winner was accustomed to meters. He quickly did the conversion. There was no problem. 138 yards perfectly equated to 126 meters.

Shortly after Bernhard hit his second shot, his veteran caddie arrived with a putter. Ryan was relieved of duty after only half a hole.

Bernhard emptied his bag with gifts. His temporary caddie rejected the generous offer of a dozen balls.

"Please keep them," Ryan said. "You might need them." They laughed.

Ryan left the Langer team and raced back to the first tee. This time, he was greeted like a celebrity with applause as he climbed the stairs to his old seat.

How many spectators get to experience the U.S. Open inside the ropes?

33

Tiger Tees

NO ONE BROKE TEES LIKE TIGER WOODS. With a swing speed that exceeded 125 mph, tees were marshmallows. He went through wood like Paul Bunyan. Every cut was a clean slice. He did that, too, like no other.

Tiger always broke his tee. He never failed. He got great distance out of golf balls, for sure. He did with tees, too. I never measured the distance, but I swear his tees probably exceeded the world long jump record (which is nearly thirty feet).

Then, he raced off to find his ball. He was already focusing on the next shot. I was left to pick up the pieces.

For about nine hours, the first tee was my office. Naturally, I wanted the area kept neat. As starter, it was my side job keep the teeing area free of debris, including tees broken by players and left there. After players drove, most picked up their tees and pocketed them for reuse. The broken ones, I picked up the pieces and threw them away.

One day, I thought, "Maybe a junior would like a U.S. Open souvenir from Tiger."

After picking up broken tee parts, I found a youngster in the gallery. Kids were often with parents. Under the ropes I went. Parents and kids were always shocked.

"Who's your favorite player?" I asked.

The answer didn't matter. Any response was fine.

"You win!" I exclaimed. "This is Tiger's tee. It's yours. Be careful. It's sharp, and don't sell it on eBay, OK?"

Their looks were priceless. I likened their reactions to those in the TV ads when the representative for Publishers Clearing House rings the doorbell to present an oversized check to the resident.

There are hundreds of knife-sharp, broken Tiger tees out there, probably tucked away in souvenir boxes. Here's hoping those tees bring back some wonderful memories of a nice, family experience at the U.S. Open.

34

Cue Tee

WHEN THE TELEVISION GOT MORE INVOLVED IN MAJOR CHAMPIONSHIPS, the official start of a round didn't always come from my inexpensive watch.

Whether it was Andy North, Roger Maltbie, or Mark Rolfing, the main walking announcers who followed big-name groups simply got the direction from their director, then pointed an index finger in my direction. That was my "go" signal.

The hand-off to me wasn't always easy. There was plenty of activity. While Roger and Mark listened intently to instructions on their headsets from a director, I was trying to stay focused.

When Dottie Pepper joined NBC's Open team in 2005, she got the assignment of cueing me. We had a little private chat.

"Dottie, let's not have any more false starts," I said. False starts were those times I mistakenly started early or even a few seconds late. "When you're ready, whack me."

So Dottie stood there, right next to me. When she got the word, I got a quick whack.

Our system worked perfectly.

35

Keeping It Open to All

T HE U.S. OPEN IS DIFFERENT. Since 1895, it has been our National Championship. It is the property of the United States Golf Association, whose shareholders are member golf clubs across the country. It might be golf's most democratic event to gain entry, and it should be.

For decades, 156 players have advanced to compete. With golf a worldwide game today, it is increasingly challenging to determine the best way to fill those precious spots. But every player who tees it up in the U.S. Open gets there one of three ways: by competing in *both* stages of qualifying, competing in *only* the second phase, or by receiving an *exemption from all qualifying* and advancing directly into the championship.

To understand how the 156-player field is determined, it probably is most easily understood by working backward.

The USGA writes a set of conditions in which players are automatically in the Open field once they send in their entry application early in the year.

The champion, for example, is exempt from all qualifying for each of the next ten years. The winners of the other three men's professional majors do not have to play in either stage of Open qualifying for five years, and the USGA recognizes those who are generally considered as the elite players in the world and permits them to bypass all qualifying. These, among other conditions, are the year's top money-winners on the PGA Tour, anyone finishing in the top fifteen from the previous year's Open, and the top players in the world rankings.

When the list of players earning full exemptions is complete, approximately half of the 156-player field is filled.

Next, the USGA lists conditions under which players are required only to play in thirty-six holes of Sectional Qualifying, scheduled at approximately ten to twelve sites around the U.S. the week before the championship proper, or at one site in England and one in Japan in May.

Those who fall into this group are highly talented players by virtually everyone's standards, but, for any number of reasons, are less than an obvious certainty to be considered among the world's elite golfers. This group would include the remaining players who have full playing privileges on the PGA Tour; players who have won major championships outside the five- or ten-year window of full-exempt status; and a large number of successful tour professionals on other tours around the world, etc.

With approximately half the starting field fully exempt, that leaves more than nine thousand players trying to get one of the remaining spots. With roughly six hundred players competing in only Sectional Qualifying, the longest of the long shots are required to advance through both stages of qualifying.

Some have opined that the U.S. Open has the weakest field among the majors. With fewer than one percent advancing to the National Championship, the premise deserves to be challenged.

Occasionally, players withdraw from the Open. Determining who gets to fill those valued spots is arduous.

Today, vacancies are filled using *two* systems. They work concurrently, thus making them somewhat complicated.

System One is hereby named the *Sectional* System.

Assume there are twelve Sectional Qualifying sites and one is in California. If a player from the California Sectional qualifies for the U.S. Open, but then withdraws, his spot is filled by the first alternate from the California Sectional site. If the first alternate declines the spot, the second alternate is offered the spot, and on down the line.

System Two is the *Reallotment* System.

It is necessary because half of the field is already fully exempt. Thus, the Sectional System cannot be applied.

If, for example, the defending champion were to withdraw, there would be no Sectional site to fill the spot because he was exempt from all qualifying.

His spot would be filled by the Reallotment System. The twelve Sectional sites are put into a numerical order—1 through 12. The order is said to be determined by preference, first to the site at which it was hardest to qualify. Again, an example helps in understanding.

If the Florida Sectional had 50 players and two qualified, there was a four percent chance, If California was next hardest with 100 players and five qualifiers, there was a five percent chance. If England had 50 players and 12 qualified, it presumably would be the "easiest" site. Therefore, Florida would be No. 1 on the Reallotment list, California second, and England far down the list. With the defending champion's withdrawal, the first alternate in Florida would get his spot. That alternate would have a prime starting time on TV, too.

No one knows when a withdrawal is going to happen.

Time can be short, perhaps less than five minutes. The lucky alternate must be correctly identified by applying the correct one of the two systems. He must be located and ready for play with clubs and caddie. Then, he must race to the correct tee—1 or 10, which can be some distance away—and be ready to play—with no warmup. The scene can be hectic.

I tried, several times, to simplify the process to some degree. My suggestion was to meld the Sectional and Reallotment Systems into one by lot, but the concept was never adopted.

Nobody ever said any democratic process came, preserved, or changed easily—even that of the U.S. Open.

36

1985: How Would You Like to Play in the U.S. Open?

IT WAS THAT NERVOUS HOUR BEFORE THE START OF THE 1985 U.S. OPEN AT OAKLAND HILLS. There was the normal excitement of the National Championship's starting day among players and officials. As we scurried in preparation, the phone in the USGA office rang.

It was a woman who identified herself as the wife of tour professional Bob Tway. She said Bob was ill with the flu and would have to withdraw. Little did I realize how this call would change my day, nor did I know we were about to make U.S. Open history.

After the call, we made several follow-up phone calls to confirm Tway's ill health. Mrs. Tway's call was not a prank; Bob indeed was bedridden and would not compete.

Previously, vacancies went unfilled after the Championship had begun. If a player dropped out after starting play, the remaining 155 players would compete. This was the protocol for eighty-four previous U.S. Opens.

The best that anyone could remember, yes, the USGA had summoned alternates in previous years, but it was done only on the days leading up to the first day. Alternates usually needed a day or two to make travel arrangements. That was all about to change.

This time was to be different. Staff leaders Frank Hannigan and P. J. Boatwright Jr. huddled.

"P. J., let's fill the spot," Hannigan said. Frank had caught the steely Boatwright at a particularly good moment. Hannigan somehow convinced P. J. to break tradition. A decision had to be made quickly. Who would be the lucky golfer among thousands who wanted Tway's spot? No other alternate was at Oakland Hills. Just as importantly, could one get through heavy Detroit traffic to even get there in time?

"Ron, get Jeff Rivard's phone number, pronto, and find out who the alternates in Michigan were," Hannigan ordered. "And, by the way, the player's starting time is at 7:36."

"Thanks, Boss," I thought. I had ninety minutes.

Jeff Rivard had conducted the qualifying for the Open as executive director of the Golf Association of Michigan. I had no idea where Rivard lived, let alone what his phone number was. A staffer found his address in suburban Ypsilanti, and I dialed 411 information. Those old rotary phones took their time. At 6:15 A.M., the ring from my call startled Rivard.

"Jeff, who were your alternates?" I blurted, getting right to the point after telling him who was calling. "And, oh yeah, good morning."

I quickly explained the reason for my hasty call.

Rivard could recite quotes of W. C. Fields and Will Rogers for hours, but this request caught him off guard. He finally cited three names in no correct order of their finish or score.

"There's no way they could get to Oakland Hills by 7:36," he opined.

We were in 100 percent uncharted territory, without a map or any rules.

"I think Randy Erskine was our fourth alternate," Jeff surmised. "He's from Ann Arbor, about forty-five miles from the club. He might make it."

It was worth a shot. I thanked Jeff. While he went back to sleep, I again sought information in Ann Arbor. A real person at 411 answered, not a computerized voice, and quickly found Erskine's number. I had a little over an hour to perform a miracle.

One ring. Two rings. Three rings. "Hello," said a voice, certainly surprised by a call at 6:20 A.M.

"Randy Erskine, please!" I urgently asked.

"This is Randy."

"Randy, this is Ron Read of the USGA," I offered. "What are you doing?"

"I'm having cereal," he responded to my stupid question.

"How would you like to play in the U.S. Open?" I could only imagine his shock.

"Your starting time is at 7:36. Can you make it?" I asked.

I later learned he thought my call was a joke being played by a local radio broadcaster. Because of his skepticism, Erskine began peppering me with questions that only one familiar with the U.S. Open might answer accurately. I passed Erskine's pop quiz.

"I'll make it," he said. "Thank you."

Randy had sixty-five minutes, in morning rush-hour traffic, to make it to the first tee.

For me, it would be a hectic hour, too. Randy would need everything—a caddie, a locker, and, perhaps most importantly, a credential. I envisioned him screeching his car to halt at the club's gate and telling the security detail, "I'm playing in the U.S. Open. Please let me in."

"Yeah, sure," might be the response.

One by one, I tried to anticipate and address the issues. First, I found him a club caddie. By the start of the Open, any caddie who did not have a bag certainly did not expect to get one. But the news of Erskine's arrival brought new excitement to the caddie shack, where several caddies still held out a glimmer of hope. One now beamed. He had a bag in the U.S. Open.

"What happens if Erskine somehow shows up with his own caddie?" I pondered. I'd faced that issue before—a player with two caddies. I kept that prospect quietly to myself and prayed it didn't happen.

Getting a player the proper credentials was the easy part. A player's badge with proper, personal engraving would have to wait.

I alerted the media center of the latest developments, and the anticipation of Randy Erskine's appearance had become a media event. Writers and TV cameras lined the entrance. If only our hero would appear!

While all this was going on, the speedometer of Erskine's car registered eighty-five mph. He admitted later that he'd buried the needle.

There's no greater privilege than to start players at the Old Course at St. Andrews. (All photos in this section provided by Ron Read.)

Left photo: Katrina made Clint's day.

Right photo: Jim Thorpe thought the USGA was trying to penalize him before he had played a shot.

Arnold, "Let's have coffee." A magical morning at Pebble Beach.

Jack didn't look like "the greatest ever" en route to an 82 at Pebble Beach.

The stunning beauty and challenge of the Pacific Northwest's first U.S Open site, Chambers Bay.

While Bob Hope paid tribute to his friend Bing Crosby, the Game owes so much to Bob and Bing.

A special evening with Arnold Palmer, Tom Watson, and Jack Nicklaus, and a drop-in—Bob Hope (see above photo).

Sir Nick Faldo accidentally spilled coffee on Katrina's nose. She vowed to never wash it off.

Arnold gave fans what they came to see at Cherry Hills.

Three-time U.S. Open Champion Hale Irwin forgot to sign his scorecard at Medinah. Yes, that's me on the right.

1983 U.S. Open participant Forrest Fezler drew the ire of P. J. Boatwright, but, technically, he didn't break any rules when he jumped into a port-a-john to change into shorts in the middle of his round.

Golf's consummate volunteer, Paul Caruso Jr., on the right. That's me on the left.

Left: There's none better than Roger Maltbie, here with Katrina.

Right: You never know whom you might run into at Pebble Beach, even Jordan Spieth.

Left: The best Father's Day gift ever, worn every championship Sunday after 1989.

Architect Robert Trent Jones Jr. at Chambers Bay GC.

The Big Crosby Tournament, which was contested at the Old Course at St. Andrew's.

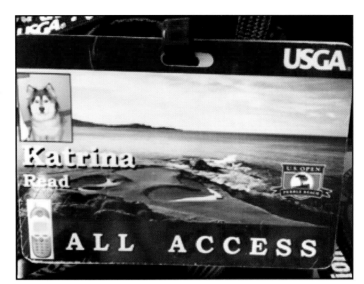

Katrina had all access at the 2010 U.S. Open.

Left: I was reunited at the St Jude-FEDEX with the last player I introduced—2010 U.S. Open champion Graeme McDowell.

The $39 watch that started the U.S. Open for 23 years.

Missy Read could rip the drive before turning to tennis.

Right: Bob Hollister represents the thousands of volunteers who gave selflessly to the Game.

Left: I'm joined by my good friend, Dottie Pepper, and our great mutual friend, Katrina.

"I know I was going over a hundred," he said. "I drove in the service lane of the freeway for safety." Miraculously, the only police officer he ever saw was at the front gate at Oakland Hills.

At 7:27, Erskine appeared with nine minutes to spare. He was already in golf spikes. He had changed his shoes in the middle of the road while waiting at a stoplight about a mile from the club.

"I'm Randy Erskine," he told the police officer.

"Yes, I know," said the kindly officer. "Come with me."

Cameras rolled. The press had their story, one that only got better.

Without a practice round or a warm-up swing, Erskine was introduced to the other two players in his group, Bill Sanders and Lindy Miller.

Erskine took three practice swings, several deep breaths, and was then introduced to thousands who had no idea what his last ninety minutes had been like.

He made a three-putt bogey on the first hole, not surprisingly. His score for the day was a 5-over par 76, amazing, really, on the course Hogan named The Monster. He shot 73 the next day, his two-day total of 149 tying or beating several big names, among them Nicklaus, Crenshaw, Langer, and Stadler. Under the circumstances, it might well have been one of the greatest ever. While that can be argued, one thing is indisputable. Randy Erskine made history in the U.S. Open.

37

Hope Springs Eternal

L IKE THE MASTERS, U.S. OPEN ATTENDANCE FIGURES ARE NEVER OFFICIALLY AN-
NOUNCED.

My guess is that 60,000 attended the 2002 U.S. Open at Bethpage Black and again at Chambers Bay in 2015, the Pacific Northwest's first U.S. Open. These are "best-guess" estimates, and they include about 45,000 spectators, 3,000 members of the media, 5,000 volunteers, players (plus their managers, swing coaches, sports psychologists, and family) caddies, security, VIPs, USGA and club staffs, volunteer officials, and perhaps the most critical group of all—the turf grass management staff and about 200 superintendents who volunteer from around the world.

The U.S. Open is a special lifetime of memories event for most. My career included thirty-three of those memories.

For a tiny group, their attendance at the Open is a period of excruciating anxiety. That condition lasts from the time they arrive until qualifier No. 156 plays in the final group on Thursday.

This small group consists of the alternates. For whatever reason, they came agonizingly close to earning one of 156 precious spots, but they came up short one week before the Open, in Sectional Qualifying.

A small number of alternates take chances. They show up at the Open with only one thing—hope. While 156 golfers dutifully prepare for the National Championship, alternates bide their time, awaiting word they are in the Open. That good news seldom comes.

Their chances are greater the week before the U.S. Open, when Sectional Qualifying is held. That's usually when unforeseen schedule changes, injuries, or personal issues arise. Further, USGA now saves several spots for unanticipated circumstances.

Once the week of the Open arrived, chances for alternates grew slim. There were always rumors of injuries or circumstances that might cause someone to withdraw. As player liaison, I didn't snoop when rumors surfaced, but I listened, then shared that information with my associates. It was a heads-up on what might happen. Rumors were never shared with alternates. Alternates, too, heard the rumors, then they hounded me.

"What are my chances?" they'd asked.

"You'll be first to know," I patently answered.

The original field of 156 was usually intact on Day One, and they all started.

When golfer No. 156 teed off on Thursday, there were long faces because at that point, it was no longer possible to make changes to the field.

Rumors occasionally proved partially true. Every player wanted to play four rounds in the U.S. Open. Some, however, did lose interest after opening rounds of 80 or higher.

There were rare times, however, when contractual commitments motivated a few to tee it up, though doubting they could compete at a high level for four days. In those rare occasions, it was exasperating for everybody—to the player who might have a nagging injury, to the alternate, and even to me. I knew how desperately alternates wanted to compete.

Alternates bear considerable expenses of airfare and lodging. They quickly learned they had no special status; until they were officially admitted into the field, there was no courtesy car, hospitality privileges, or complimentary tickets that go to each player. They were not permitted to play practice rounds, and they were not assigned lockers, which vendors stuff with new clubs, balls, gloves, bags, and clothing.

Alternates could hit balls when space was available. They were permitted to putt and to walk the course.

The plight of one alternate remains fresh in my mind.

Alex Prugh, nineteen, was a sophomore at the University of Washington. He was the first alternate from around the nation on the USGA's reallotment list, which notes the order of alternates after Sectional Qualifying. He came to Shinnecock Hills in 2004.

I knew Alex was a gambler. That was clear on the final hole at Sectional Qualifying in Washington. Believing he needed a birdie or better to advance to Shinnecock Hills, he attempted to drive the green from 325 yards. It was a risky decision. Luckily, we found his drive near a water hazard, but a well-earned, difficult par left him one stroke short of qualifying.

The following week, the young alternate took another chance. He traveled to the U.S. Open with his mother, Sue. They flew from their home in Spokane to New York, then drove to Long Island on the Monday of U.S. Open week.

Hotels in the area required a week's stay at premium rates. They could not make a commitment for seven evenings, so they hopscotched between two hotels, each an hour's commute, best case, from Shinnecock Hills.

Only one thing was free for Alex, his caddie. Mom was prepared to carry his heavy bag.

On Tuesday, Alex learned he could not play the course, but he could walk it. He spotted Tiger headed for a late practice round. So, he tagged along inside the ropes. On the second hole, a large man picked Alex out of the entourage and escorted him outside the ropes, underscoring his limited status as an alternate. Even Tiger's security detail knew that.

At 6:00 on Thursday morning, Team Prugh beat heavy traffic and arrived in time for the 7 A.M. start. While Alex putted, Sue checked in at the USGA rules trailer. No one had withdrawn. Sue did not stop there. She descended on me, setting up the first tee at 6:30.

"Has anybody dropped out?" she asked.

"I am sorry, Sue," I said that with empathy a dozen more times throughout the day.

At 1:07, an alarm was sounded that gave hope. Jim Farrell, the starter on the tenth tee, radioed that Toshimitsu Izawa was missing. With less than a minute until the 1:10 starting time, Jim called again, still panicked and missing Toshi.

I had alerted Sue and Alex after Jim's first call, and they went running to the tenth tee. Mom tried to keep up, packing clubs. They arrived just in time to see Toshi dip under the ropes. They were about twenty seconds from being in the U.S. Open.

There were two other what-if moments for the Prughs. Carlos Franco played four holes, then withdrew, while David Duval went nine holes before heading home.

The Prughs stayed at Shinnecock Hills until the last starting time on Thursday. To them the place might forever be known as Heartbreak Hills Golf Club, but to their lasting credit, they never gave up hope.

38

One Too Many

THE FIRST PLAYER TO BE INTRODUCED AT SHINNECOCK IN 2004 WAS J. J. HENRY. After introducing J. J. to referee Stan Grossman and observer Ken Adler, Father's Day greetings were extended to all in this collegial group.

With a few minutes to wait before J. J.'s start, we had time to chat. Stan brought up the coming U.S. Senior Amateur at Bel Aire Country Club the following October. Bel Aire is a special place in Los Angeles, and the club has a storied past. This Senior Amateur was of particular importance to me. I was involved in facilitating the invitation to host the event. Any mention of Bel Aire brought to mind the name of my friend—J. J. Wagner, its CEO and general manager.

Our free time was over. It was now time for the 8:40 A.M. starting time.

"Ladies and gentlemen, from Fairfield, Connecticut, please welcome… J. J. *Wagner*."

My friend was still asleep some 2,500 miles to the west, but he was now introduced to play in the U.S. Open!

There was a murmur. I sensed something was wrong. I looked up to hear this J. J., very much awakened, perhaps by my latest faux pas. He was chuckling along with the large audience. Once again, my use of the word "Correction" was needed.

The following February, in 2005, J. J. Henry played in the A.T.&T Pebble Beach National Pro-Am. He was socializing with country music star Clay Walker, and J. J. summoned me over so he could retell this story. We're still laughing.

39

Sometimes, It Pays to Take the Call

M Y FRIEND LARRY ADAMSON ACCEPTED MORE THAN FIFTY THOUSAND ENTRIES A YEAR FOR NATIONAL CHAMPIONSHIPS CONDUCTED BY THE USGA. In his twenty-four years doing this , he took many calls about those events. Larry called them "Sad, Glad, and Mad Calls." Some golfers were sad, especially when they had to withdraw. Others were glad when they were told their entries had arrived at Golf House on time. Many were very mad, often when they'd received the infamous "black list letter," advising them their entries would not be accepted next year because of poor play in attempting to qualify.

One of the sad calls found Larry listening to a fellow who faced a hardship causing him to withdraw from the second stage of qualifying for the U.S. Open—the Sectional.

The good news was that Larry now would get to make a "glad" call. The year was 1984. He would have to call and advise the first alternate from a stage one—Local—qualifying site that he was now eligible to fill the vacant spot. Larry enjoyed delivering the good news. It was always a happy occasion on both ends of the telephone line.

Larry rang the first alternate, a sixteen-year-old, who most certainly would accept his invitation. It was the dad who took Larry's call, since the boy was still in school. First, Larry identified himself as being from the Championship Department at the USGA.

111

"Do you accept the position in Sectional Qualifying?" Larry asked the father. He already knew the answer.

"Yes….yes…YES!" Dad excitedly responded, but he had a few questions for Larry.

" Are you sure you are who you say you are?" Dad was suspicious. Then he added, "Are you sure of what you are telling me?"

Larry answered those questions, twice each, before the father finally believed him. Now Larry could fill him in on the details.

"Do you know his pairing?" Dad asked. "Who's he playing with?"

"Yes," the USGA good Samaritan said. "Arnold Palmer."

There was a long pause, followed by laughter.

"No, really . . . Who is he playing with?"

"He is paired with Arnold Palmer."

There was now a really long pause.

"Are you really serious?"

"Yes."

"My son's only sixteen years old!"

Larry's surprise was beginning to sink in.

"What's he going to do? He'll be scared to death."

Larry finally convinced Dad that everything would be fine and that it would be a special experience.

Do you think?

By this time in his career, Arnie was no longer exempt into the Open, but true to his nature, he was going to try, just like nine thousand others.

The day after Sectional Qualifying, Larry took a call from the boy's father.

"Mr. Adamson, I had to call," he said. "I can't tell you what an experience our son . . . well, in fact, the whole family had yesterday. . . How kind. . . how nice Mr. Palmer was to our son. As our son came to the (first) tee, Mr. Palmer went to him, introduced himself, and told him, 'Young man, just play your game, enjoy this day and time. You'll be fine.'"

Dad broke down.

"What a nice man," he managed to finally say. "What a day he made for our son . . . What a memory. . . What a memory he gave to all of us."

"Sometimes, the best thing we can give or receive in life," Larry told me, "is a good memory."

Arnold Palmer did that for all.

40

Roger Maltbie: Taken for a Ride

ROGER MALTBIE IS A CONSTANT IN MY LIFE. HIS DISPOSITION NEVER CHANGES. He's always been fun-loving and enjoyable to be around, and he remains one of golf's nicest guys. Always has been, always will be.

In 1971, I watched him defeat Dallan Ragland, 3 and 2, to win the Northern California Golf Association Amateur at Spyglass Hill Golf Club. He wore red plaid double-knit slacks that would make John Daly blush. His waist size was less than the number of holes he played that day—thirty-four—and he had fun every step of the way.

Roger went on to win five times on the PGA Tour.

He was best known for winning Jack Nicklaus's first Memorial Tournament in 1976 in a four-hole playoff with Hale Irwin. In the celebration that followed, he had such a good time that he left the $40,000 winner's check in the bar.

There's irony in Roger's U.S. Open career. He had greater success as an on-course commentator for NBC at twenty U.S. Opens, but he had limited achievement in the eight times he played in the U.S. Open. His best finish was thirty-second in 1983.

He did not qualify for the 1985 U.S. Open at Oakland Hills Country Club, but he set a scoring record while trying. Well, it was a record of sorts.

When he arrived at the qualifying site in Maryland, Roger was pleasantly surprised to hear USGA had eased rules by allowing players to use golf carts. Where he got that information, who knows? But with the prospect of walking thirty-six holes, he welcomed the ride.

On the ninth hole, Tom Meeks, the USGA staff member overseeing the conduct of the qualifier, spotted Roger riding to the green. When Roger was done playing the hole, Tom asked him how he'd scored on first nine holes.

"I'm even par—36," Roger said.

"How many holes did you ride?" Tom asked

"Uh . . .Let's see… Beginning at four . . . five . . . six . . ." Roger began to count. "Six holes on the front side. Why?"

"Roger, make that score 48, not 36," Meeks said.

Carts were, in fact, prohibited. The penalty, at that time, was two strokes per hole. Thus, Roger incurred what is believed to be the only twelve-stroke penalty in the history of golf.

Good-natured Maltbie handed the historic scorecard to Tom, got in his car and drove across D.C, to the hotel, where his wife, Donna, was still sleeping. He slipped back into the bed he'd left a few hours earlier.

"What are you doing here?" she asked.

He explained what had happened.

Six years later, he joined NBC's golf telecast team. In 1995, at Shinnecock, he became my boss before special starting times. He cued me to start "featured groups" on the broadcast.

When Maltbie appeared on the first tee, something important was about to happen.

"I'm baaaaacccccccck!" he would wail.

When Roger appeared in 2009 at Bethpage Black, I knew something was up. He was ready for action, fully equipped with a large backpack that carried electronic gear, and a headset that allowed him to communicate with those in charge of the broadcast. He was smiling, but something didn't seem quite right.

The networks, I knew, only accompanied groups with familiar names and the next group on my pairing sheet was not one of those.

"Roger, who are you going out with?" I asked.

"Tiger."

I looked at the pairing sheet. The Bethpage Open was plagued by rain and there were countless changes. But there was no change in the next group.

"Roger, I have some bad news," I said. "Tiger starts on number 10."

His eyes got really big, about the size of silver dollars.

Tiger played in five minutes and the 10th tee was nowhere near the first. Roger had to be there. NBC's director and producer certainly were counting on it.

"Roger, I can solve your problem," I said.

A New York State Trooper was nearby.

"Officer," I said. "Roger must be at the tenth tee in four minutes. Can you help, please?"

Before he hustled to the officer's car, I said, "Roger, if you get there in time, you owe me a jar of mayonnaise." Again, there was a smile.

Off they sped. They had a near accident with NBC's Al Roker, whose golf cart would have lost to the speeding patrol car.

But Roger made his assignment, thanks to the officer.

Why a reward of mayonnaise?

Shortly before that Open, I had called the Maltbie home. Donna answered. Roger was not there. He was shopping at his favorite place—Costco.

"Call him," she said.

I was calling Roger to learn about his unique experience in 2002, when he was asked by NBC executive producer Tommy Roy to get a starting time in the true Bethpage fashion—by getting there in the middle of the night and standing in line. Tommy wanted a piece on what it was like to stand in that line for a tee time.

So, the afternoon before he hoped to play, Roger drove to Long Island, joined a long line of cars in his rented Winnebago RV and waited all night, as legions of golfers did every weekend. Roger played cards, drank beer, and made new friends until the starter's office opened at sunrise the next morning.

When I called, I was now as curious about his shopping mission as I was his all-night experience at Bethpage. He took my call.

"Roger, where are you?"

"I'm at Costco."

"What are you buying?" I asked.

"I'm loading mayonnaise on a skid."

The visual of Roger Maltbie roaming the aisles of the busy market, loading mayonnaise—and certainly libations—on a skid, while signing autographs and visiting friends, was more than I could handle.

I'm still waiting for the mayo.

41

Newton's Favorite Golf Rule Was Mine, Too

ALTON MCEWEN'S TWENTY-FOOT PUTT HUNG ON THE LIP OF THE SIXTEENTH HOLE, in a friendly game of golf. The ball peeked into the hole. He got close to the ball, breathed heavily, and growled something inaudible or unprintable.

This was déja vu. I went into my rules mode and began to count for Alton. "One second, two seconds . . ." But when I got to six, gravity took over and the ball fell into the bottom of the hole. We laughed. Isaac Newton was looking down, chortling, too.

This was at Quail Golf Club in Carmel, California, in 2018.

Seeing this caused another flashback for me, taking me back to the 1985 Open at Oakland Hills Country Club, outside of Detroit, Michigan, where Andy North was to win his second Open. He finished one stroke ahead of three others—Dave Barr of Canada, T. C. Chen of Taiwan, and Denis Watson of Zimbabwe. Each had his chance. Out of those, only Barr avoided a brush with the rules.

Barr led with six holes to play, but then he bogeyed three holes down the stretch.

Chen incurred a one-stroke penalty on the fifth hole, where he struck a chip shot twice in one swing. The penalty earned T. C. the nickname "Two-Chip Chen," although the 2019 changes to the rules removed the one-stroke penalty.

Watson also experienced rules infamy.

Like McEwen's, Watson's ball eventually fell into the eighth hole. Unlike Alton, Watson suffered bad luck.

Denis had a en-foot putt for a par four, but the ball stopped on the hole's edge.

What happened then remained vivid in my memory, though I was not on the scene.

Instead, P. J. Boatwright Jr. and I were in the rules office getting a live report.

Referee Montford T. Johnson III radioed to P. J. He excitedly related that Watson's ball was on the hole's lip. Denis raced to the hole, where he eyed the ball from close range, hoping his laser-like stare might cause it to fall. He waited. And waited. And waited.

Johnson was a smart guy, an Annapolis grad, now a full-time cattle rancher in Amarillo, Texas, and he was a part-time rules official. He knew his limitations under these frantic circumstances. He tried to keep P. J. up-to-date, second-by-second, with a description of what was taking place during Watson's staredown. P. J. radioed back to M.T., but they were apparently speaking at the same time. M.T. never got P. J.'s message.

"Tell him to hit it!" P. J. repeated it several times.

Later, we calculated Watson stared at the ball for about forty seconds. P. J.'s transmission finally reached M. T. He instructed the official to tell Watson to add two strokes to his score on the hole for "undue delay."

Just as P. J.'s communication reached Johnson, the ball fell into the hole.

The situation highlighted a dilemma for a player at that time. The rules prohibited players from hitting a moving ball. Players all knew that, and they always waited, claiming the ball was still moving. At the same time, they hoped for the best—the ball eventually falling into the cup. There were occasions when players waited several minutes while, behind them, others waited. After the Watson incident in an event broadcast around the world, some kind of action was needed.

Enter two of the best thinkers in the game—C. Grant Spaeth and Frank Hannigan.

Spaeth was chairman of the Championship Committee and Hannigan was USGA executive director. They realized an overhaul was necessary. They collaborated to change what then was Rule 16-2, and they removed the player's dilemma.

Under their revision, when a ball overhung the hole, a player was allowed a reasonable time to walk to the hole, without dawdling. A player then had an additional ten seconds to assess the ball's status—moving or motionless. After ten seconds, the ball was deemed to be at rest. If the ball fell in during those ten seconds, it was considered holed with the last stroke. But if the ball fell into the hole after ten seconds, the penalty was one stroke, not two as was assessed to Watson. The player's dilemma for playing a moving ball was gone. Further, the new rule eliminated incentive to delay play further.

They found a solution to an age-old problem. Some will say the Committee violated its own rule of "undue delay," but practical solutions often take time.

42

The Dreamers, and One of the Best U.S. Open Stories of All Time

I T MIGHT BE CALLED GOLF'S LOTTO—ATTEMPTING TO QUALIFY FOR THE U.S. OPEN.
The odds are slim, but that doesn't seem to matter.

Every spring, as regular as swallows returning to Capistrano, thousands of men—and the occasional woman—give it a try.

By definition in the U.S. Open entry application, they are all exceptional golfers: professionals or amateurs who have handicap indexes of 1.4 or less.

When the second of the two qualifying stages rolls around, there generally are about half the spots in the field of 156 available in that year's U.S. Open. Fighting for them are customarily some 8,000-10,000 talented and optimistic players.

My sentiments will always be with the dreamers who face the challenge of trying to get into our Open through two stages of qualifying. They exemplify the true spirit of the U.S. Open.

One such dreamer was a Hawaiian trying to qualify for the first time. He entered at Poipu Bay Golf Course on the island of Kauai. He approached me after being introduced on the first tee. He said, "I've been dreaming of this moment since I was a little boy."

His dream did not come true. In fact, it ended early. He could not find his first tee shot.

Another was a young man who entered at Rio Secco Golf Club near Las Vegas. It was his second attempt. He reminded me that I had started him the year before at a qualifier near Reno, Nevada. He was so excited on that occasion that he left his car running—all day. After failing to qualify, his first task was to fill an empty gas tank.

And there was Dr. Jim Rheim, my dermatologist.

When he asked my prediction, I suggested that he play the final nine holes at Almaden Golf and Country Club under par to have a chance of qualifying. He did—two under—to advance to the 1977 U.S. Open at Southern Hills.

Hubert Green won that Open and Dr. Jim finished 156th—last. Jim does hold a record, though. Through 2018, he's the last medical doctor to play in the U.S. Open.

There is no shortage of dreamers.

Darrell Kestner qualified for the 2002 at Bethpage State Park's Black Course, near his home club of Deepdale.

Prior to the first round, I introduced Darrell, thirty-eight, to fellow competitor Derek Tolan, sixteen. Derek knew nothing about Darrell, only his name. After their introduction, Derek asked Darrell, "This your first Open?"

Darrell paused, then smiled. He humbly responded, "No, my eighth."

I'm not certain the young lad actually said it, but his look definitely did say, "Why haven't I heard of you?"

Between 1979 at Inverness and 2002, Kestner had qualified eight times, advancing through both stages each and every time. If that's not a record, it should be. Darrell followed his dream for those twenty-three years.

Then there was a young man who set another record in his first U.S. Open.

"You don't know what pressure is," Lee Trevino said, "until you play for five bucks with only two dollars in your pocket," but Andy Dillard might have seconded Lee's comment.

Dillard's pressure was also financial. He arrived at the 1992 U.S. Open at Pebble Beach with $50.

The Oklahoman knew golf's tough times. He missed qualifying for the U.S. Open in 1991 by one stroke. His misfortune was the result of bad planning. He had not played a practice round. Not knowing the course, he played straight-away to a green on a par-4. The problem was, it was the wrong green. The correct green was to the right on the dogleg hole. Bad judgment cost him a trip at Hazeltine.

Andy planned better in 1992. He advanced through Local Qualifying in Oklahoma City, near his home. Then, he jumped into his truck and drove to Memphis. He was successful in Sectional Qualifying there.

Given his poor financial situation, he needed good news, and he got it.

At the conclusion of the PGA Tour event played the week before the U.S. Open, the FedEx St. Jude Classic in Memphis, Tennessee, players were flown to Pebble Beach.

Once there, Dillard knew $50 in his pocket would not go far.

"All I could think about was money," Andy confided. "Winning the Open trophy was never on my mind. My only goal was to make the cut. There was a $1,000 payout if we made it to the third round. I was motivated, for sure."

On Tuesday, Andy wrote a check for $1,500. There was one problem. He had no money in the bank.

As one of two officials empowered to authorize players' checks of that size, I had approved the check for the local bank to cash!

"Given my state of mind, I was pretty relaxed Thursday morning on the first tee," he said. "I was paired with Bob Estes and Tom Jenkins. I remember my start like it was yesterday."

If he was nervous, he did not show it.

"From Edmond, Oklahoma . . . Andy Dillard," I said at 10:31.

He struck a solid first shot, then hit a seven-iron to ten feet. His putt hit the center of the hole for a birdie. At No. 2, his chip lipped out for an eagle but left him a short putt for another birdie. Then he birdied the third and the name Dillard was now on top of every leaderboard.

News spread rapidly. The gallery grew. They may have been whispering, "Who's Andy Dillard?"

He added three more birdies at 4, 5 and 6. No one had ever opened with six birdies in the previous ninety-one U.S. Opens.

The record was impressive. However, the bigger news was the fact that a relative unknown, one who was a qualifier through two stages, was leading the U.S. Open!

But was Andy done with his birdie barrage?

A sizable crowd joined him on the Pebble's incomparable holes, the short par-3 seventh and the great par-4 eighth. There was buzz aplenty. They were witnessing history. He struck a 15-footer badly at the seventh, then missed a downhill 3-footer for birdie on No. 8, He could have had eight straight birdies!

Andy finished with 68 that day, then had 70 on Friday. He was paired in the final group on Saturday with the leader, Gil Morgan, who was a close friend of Dillard. They both were from Edmond, Oklahoma.

Together, they struggled. Andy's 79 was two strokes higher than Gil's 77. Under windy conditions on Sunday, Andy carded 77, tying him for seventeenth. If he had finished one stroke lower, he would have been exempt into the following year's U.S. Open at Baltusrol Golf Club in New Jersey. He also would have qualified for the Masters, another lifelong dream.

In addition to the $18,069 he earned, Dillard's ball sponsor added $23,000 for all the TV exposure Titleist received. It was found money in Andy's magical U.S. Open odyssey. With his bank account now flush, Andy flew back to Memphis, commercially this time.

I'm sure he didn't think that was a problem. At least he could retrieve his truck out of long-term parking back in Memphis.

* * *

Perhaps no dreamer had a greater impact on me than Henry J. Brown.

His story was again shared by Larry Adamson, who worked for the USGA for more than two decades, accepting and processing the estimated fifty thousand entries submitted annually for the association's thirteen national championships.

Keep in mind, this was in the day before smartphones and mobile apps. Players who wanted to enter a USGA championship had three options with their paper application: put a stamp on an envelope and hand it off to the U.S. Postal Service; show up at the USGA headquarters (Far Hills, New Jersey) in person (this was a popular choice on the day applications were due); or send it via an overnight delivery service.

In twenty-four years at the USGA, Adamson received many unusual appeals. Many were from those whose entries were received after the 5:00 P.M. deadline on closing day.

That deadline was firm, and there were no exceptions. As Adamson said to more than one deadline-challenged applicant, "If I take your application five minutes late, then I have to take another (late by) ten minutes, or an hour and a half—or tomorrow."

In the spring of 1980, Adamson received a letter in the mail. What was unique about it was that the envelope and the letter inside were from stationery given to inmates at the Augusta (Georgia) city jail.

The author of the letter was Henry Jeremiah Brown. He explained that at the moment, he was behind bars for failure to make alimony payments. The letter professed his innocence, of course, and seeing as how it looked as though he might be jailed until at least August, he would be unable to participate in U.S. Open qualifying as required by all the other entrants. Then he asked Adamson if the person in charge of the conduct of the Open, P. J. Boatwright Jr., could fly to Augusta to personally accompany Henry through as much qualifying as it would take to prove his golfing prowess.

"I'll take Mr. Boatwright to the muni, The Patch," Henry said. "He'll see that I can really play even on cauliflower greens."

To further prove his desire to conduct himself on the up and up, Henry said, "If you can set up this (qualifier) for me, you can even handcuff me between shots."

Days later, Adamson wrote Henry with the bad news. There would be no special qualifier. He encouraged Henry to enter the next year, after his legal problems were resolved.

Henry J. Brown was no stranger to top-level golf. He was a caddie at Augusta National Golf Club—yes, *that* Augusta National—and often worked for Roberto de Vicenzo during the Masters. In fact, in 1968, when de Vicenzo famously missed out on a playoff because of a scorecard error, his caddie that week was none other than Henry J. Brown.

A short time after his first try to qualify for the U.S. Open went awry, Henry called Adamson. He accepted the decision in the proper spirit, and then he also shared good news. He was exonerated—a free man.

Henry returned "home"—to a junkyard near South Bend, Indiana. (Rest assured, this is all true.)

USGA volunteer Bob Lee visited what Henry called his "home office," where he also lived. Henry proudly demonstrated his golf skill on his personal "range."

"See that Chevy?" Henry would ask. Using a cross-handed grip, Henry grabbed a seven-iron and promptly hit a shot that bounced off the hood of the car. Yes, Henry really could play.

But could he follow instructions?

Henry mailed in his entry in 1981—sadly, after the deadline.

Weeks earlier he had walked into the golf shop at South Bend Country Club, where the Local Qualifier was scheduled, and said, "I'm going to win the U.S. Open."

"Before you win, Henry," head professional Banks Guyton said, "get your entry in on time."

This time, the response was the same from the USGA: Sorry, Henry. No exceptions.

"All I knew is that Henry J. Brown was the most unique character I've ever met," said John Fineran, then a sports writer for the *South Bend Tribune*. "Lee Trevino is supposed to be the ultimate hustler-in-the-Open Cinderella story. But if Henry J. had ever made it to the Open, he could have been a legend in his own right. Of all the long shots to play for the golf championship of his country, Henry would have been the longest."

Henry J. Brown didn't give up easily, and in 1982, playing in the Open was again on his mind.

We'll let a few paragraphs from the USGA's former magazine, *Golf Journal,* tell this part of the story.

The story of Henry's 1982 arrival at South Bend Country Club, and his day at the Local Qualifier has been oft-repeated.

"He came chugging up the long, sweeping driveway in his banged-up 1965 Pontiac Catalina, which had a hood ornament that used to be on either a golf or a bowling trophy," Lee remembers. "But just as he got up to the bag-drop area, one of his tires had a blowout. So he drove the car, clumpety-thumpety-clump, off to the side of the driveway and left it."

Naturally, (head professional) Banks Guyton came running out to scream at Henry. He said, "Dammit, Henry, you have that junker out of my driveway by five o'clock or I'll have it towed."

Fineran picks up the story. "Later in the day, after Henry J. had tied Tommy Stevens for first place in the qualifier, Henry was giving a TV interview and standing right in front of his disabled junker. All of a sudden, this other car came up the driveway and stopped next to him, and two good-looking women hopped out and pulled a spare tire out of their trunk and put it on Henry's old car—right in front of the TV cameras."

The remarkable story did not have a fairy tale ending. Weeks later, at Sectional Qualifying in Chicago, Henry J. Brown missed a spot in the U.S. Open at Pebble Beach by two strokes. When Adamson got the news, he called Henry to extend his condolences.

"Henry, I'm really, really sorry," Adamson said.

Henry would have none of it.

"Mr. Larry," said Henry, "don't feel sorry for me. All I ever wanted was a chance. All I ever wanted was a chance."

Henry J. Brown never got his chance in the U.S. Open. We did meet once though. He left a lasting impression,there, in his colorful attire and cross-handed style of play. More importantly, he left a lasting mark on me at every U.S. Open. After Larry Adamson told me Henry's story, I took a quiet moment before the start of every Open to reflect on what he meant to our national championship.

Henry J. Brown never got to the U.S. Open. His spirit did.

43

2002: Ben Crane: Quick to Do Good

B AD RAPS ARE LEVIED ALL THE TIME. Sometimes it's because of a misdeed. Often, it's a misspoken word.

Whatever the reason, there is no erasure, and there are seldom "mulligans" in real life. A reputation becomes how people are viewed. The characterization might not be accurate, but it still lingers.

Golfer Ben Crane received a bad rap, and deservedly so. He's been viewed as a slow player, which many believe to be one of golf's mortal sins.

That reputation, like his clubs, traveled with him to every tournament. Ben is a terrific person, though—kind, honest, and a man committed to his wonderful family. None of those qualities mattered on the golf course, where he was painfully slow.

Ben learned his deliberate pre-shot routine before he hit balls or the books at the University of Oregon. Off and on the course, he also learned what really matters in life. For this, he deserves some slack.

To view Ben Crane as only a slow player is shortsighted.

My experience dates back to Player Registration at Bethpage in 2002. The staff of Gov. George Pataki asked my help. Could a contestant meet with the children of firefighters and policemen who lost their lives on 9/11?

This Open was a historic occasion. It was New York's coming-out party—its first major event since the tragedy. Of course I would help if I could. So would the players.

The first player I asked was Ben Crane, then a rookie on the PGA Tour. Ben was a relative unknown, but he had what 8,468 others wanted—a berth in the U.S. Open. His biggest title to date had been the 1998 Pacific Coast Amateur at Eugene Country Club in Oregon. He'd shown promise as runner-up in the Byron Nelson Classic a month before this U.S. Open.

For the assignment with these kids, he did not require playing credentials—only some heart.

"Yes, I'll be happy to help," he said, and he didn't slow-play the request. We agreed to meet at 7:30 the next morning.

Ben arrived at the appointed time, but there were no children.

"No problem," he said. "I'll go putt."

Eight o'clock came and passed. So did 9:00. He continued putting.

In the meantime, Greg Norman registered ,and he took less than a nanosecond in agreeing to join the group. Now all we needed were the children.

At 10 o'clock, I ordered, "Ben, go play. This is the U.S. Open." He defied the suggestion, perhaps sensing a calling certainly higher than mine.

Finally, at 11:00 A.M., kids and officials arrived. They assembled with my new heroes—Crane and Norman. It was a lovefest. Everyone got autographs. Ben and Greg gave away nearly everything in their bags—golf gloves, balls and, most importantly, their time.

Crane posted 75-76—151 to miss the cut by one stroke. Had he practiced on-course those few extra hours, my bet is Ben would have played the final thirty-six holes. But he made no excuse.

To this day, whenever I'm looking at scores from a Tour event, I can't help it: I'm always hoping Ben plays well.

44

Bob Hollister:
He Left the Game Better

ONE OF THE BEST THINGS ABOUT SERVING THE GAME OF GOLF FOR FORTY-THREE YEARS WAS WORKING WITH THOUSANDS OF VOLUNTEERS. They gave their time and resources, freely, most often for one reason—a love for their pastime.

I was fortunate to work with them at some one hundred national championships, plus countless state, regional, and qualifying events. On those long days, many of which started before sunrise and ended after sunset, we worked side by side. Their dedication never ceased to amaze me.

After one such day in 1977, I named U.S. Open Sectional Qualifying, "Golf's Longest Day." It's thirty-six holes for golfers and much longer for those conducting it.

If there's another game that attracts more generous volunteers, I have not experienced it. Every volunteer matters. The staggering purses in professional golf would never be possible without them, nor would the thousands of amateur competitions conducted by state and regional golf associations. In the U.S. alone, the number of volunteers must be well over a hundred thousand, all giving back to golf.

Many volunteers have stood out over the years. Some became close personal friends.

Hundreds could be cited. I am singling out Bob Hollister of Tacoma, Washington, who passed away in December 2016.

We met in 1984 when Bob was general manager of Tacoma (Washington) Country & Golf Club.

Founded in 1894, TC&GC was the oldest club in the West, and it had a long tradition of hosting amateur championships—national, state, and regional. Bob saw to it that his club continued that tradition. He engineered the hosting of the 1984 U.S. Senior Women's Amateur.

Tony Zirpoli and I conducted the event in a true partnership of a great club and USGA volunteers working together. The key player was Bob. He was everywhere, doing everything, in the months preceding and during the week. His style was low key. We kidded him that he was like a mortician, always in the background, bothered by nothing but getting the job done.

Given Bob's dedication, we invited him to serve on the USGA's Regional Affairs Committee. He served selflessly for thirty years. He was truly a gift to golf, one that kept on giving, endlessly, and he did so for all the right reasons. Not once did he ever seek credit.

With TC&GC approaching its centennial year, Bob sought to make that year even more special for the club. He persuaded the board to invite the USGA for the 1994 U.S. Women's Mid-Amateur. Once again, he delivered, and his club added to its storied history of supporting amateur golf. TC&GC's generosity ranks with any.

After eighteen years at TC&GC, Bob accepted a new challenge. He became general manager at Sahalee Country Club, near Seattle, but the spirit of giving back to golf traveled with him. Sahalee hosted the 1998 PGA Championship, then the 2002 NEC World Championship. Shortly before becoming GM at nearby Overlake Golf Club, he took my call.

"Bob, we badly need a site for the 2010 U.S. Senior Open," I said.

Within a month, he delivered a Senior Open invitation to the USGA. Then, he quietly moved on to his new assignment at Overlake.

Interestingly, Bob and I attended that U.S. Senior Open as spectators, outside the ropes. The event Bob facilitated was highly successful with Seattle's Fred Couples on the leaderboard until the end. We could smile.

We often chuckled, mostly at my mistakes, on the first tee at more than twenty U.S. Opens. Bob was my gofer. He had a tough assignment—trying to make me look good. He replenished the starter's box with hole location sheets, pencils, and even new scorecards when the official ones suddenly disappeared. He often herded players and volunteer scorekeepers to prevent their lateness to the first tee.

We had a light moment in 2004 at Shinnecock Hills. A special guest arrived on the first tee. It was Prince Andrew, the Duke of York and Captain of the Royal & Ancient Golf Club of St. Andrews. He was assigned to be a special observer with the final pairing. The Prince attended the U.S. Open unannounced, and he roamed anonymously. Few knew he was in attendance. I knew only because we shared ice cream in a hospitality area. Dove Bars became the choice of royalty and a commoner.

The Prince arrived for his assignment fifteen minutes early, and I introduced him to Fred Funk and Phil Mickelson. The appearance of royalty surprised them. In response to meeting the players, the Prince humbly introduced himself simply, saying only, "Hello, I'm Andrew."

Bob observed the introductions, but he had yet to meet the him. When I finally had the chance to introduce Bob, he said to the Prince, whom he knew only as Andrew. "I'm sorry, I didn't catch . . ."

I anticipated what was on Bob's mind and quickly interrupted him.

"Bob, we need more pencils, please."

After formal introductions of Retief Goosen, Ernie Els, referee Fred Ridley, observer Walter Driver and His Royal Highness officially to the world for TV and spectators, Bob and I looked at each other and pondered.

"What is his last name?"

Only Bob could come up with the answer, "Edward."

He must have used Google.

Bob's counsel was invaluable. He and his wife, Jen, lived a few miles south of Chambers Bay, in Steilacoom, Washington. He kept me informed on a variety of local issues—course conditions at Chambers Bay and other topics, often political. He did so through the 2010 U.S. Amateur and until my departure from the USGA in 2013. He was uncannily accurate in his assessments.

Yes, we did play golf together. A highlight came on the eleventh hole, then a par-3, at the Home Course, near Chambers Bay. We both hit excellent tee shots. Both balls disappeared.

"One might be a 1," we imagined. There was, and I lost the hole with a tap-in 2. But what a way to do it.

45

2006: Jeff Sluman—The Man Deserved a Mulligan in My Book

GOLF CAN BE A SELFISH ENDEAVOR, ESPECIALLY AT THE ELITE, PROFESSIONAL LEVEL. It's a game for most, the amateurs, who play strictly for fun without remuneration; for the top professionals, it's a job. Hours are long. Family time is often short. They rank highly in all frequent flyer and hotel programs. Rewards can exceed childhood dreams, but for most, life is not as glamorous at it appears.

Jeff Sluman was highly successful playing the PGA Tour and then as a senior. Jeff and I were well-acquainted and, to me, Jeff's life had found a rare balance to be admired in any profession. He had it all. His wife, Linda, is an oncologist. They have wonderful children and successful careers. He and Linda are hugely charitable to causes in the Chicago area.

The only thing with which I could find fault was their choice of residence, the quaint and beautiful village of Hinsdale, west of Chicago. I once had a soft spot for the town. My mom was a waitress there, and we lived above the restaurant when I was a little boy. My dislike for Hinsdale came later. Hinsdale Central's Red Devils, were the rivals of my nearby high school, Lyons Township of LaGrange. Feelings of rivalry always remain. Ask Jack Nicklaus and Arnold Palmer.

The flaw of their residency aside, I knew Jeff was a solid person. When I'm asked who the nicest golfers are, Jeff is always on my short list.

I was reminded of Jeff's character while reading a piece by Jim Tunney, a former NFL official. Jim wrote about Jeff losing a playoff to Mark O'Meara years ago at Pebble Beach. Rather than pout, Jeff kept a promise. He showed up an hour later at a nearby course to fulfill a commitment to a young friend. Jeff had told the lad he'd give him a golf lesson. With a father and son already on the course, Jeff appeared at the sixteenth hole, joining the boy and his father for the last three holes. The dad said, "Jeff, you don't have to do this."

"There's nothing better for getting rid of disappointment than helping someone else," Jeff responded. This did not surprise the boy or his father. It did not surprise me, either.

Others did not yet know the Jeff Sluman I knew from many U.S. Opens.

The saying goes, "You never get a second chance to make a first impression." To some, Jeff earned one blemish at Winged Foot.

Sluman arrived at the U.S. Open at Winged Foot in 2006 on Saturday afternoon. He looked as though he'd already played thirty-six holes on a hot, sticky day. He had yet to play or practice, but that was not clear from his appearance. It was the result of a mistake.

He was to have been met at the club's entrance, then taken to Player Registration in the clubhouse. Plans went awry. The dedicated volunteer assigned to greet him was assisting another player at the appointed time. So Jeff carried his weighty tour bag, shoes, and belongings up a hill about a quarter-mile, through a throng. Fans recognized him and requested autographs. He obliged and finally hoofed it up the hill, pursued every step of the way. When he arrived at Player Registration, Jeff was not in the gentlemanly mood known well to me.

As he registered, his feelings were transparent. He was not rude, but he was not congenial, either. I did not blame him, given his circumstance.

After Player Registration closed for the day, I gathered all volunteers and conducted an informal survey. "Was anybody difficult with whom to deal?" I asked.

The result was no surprise. The vote was unanimous: Jeff was the winner, 12-0.

"That's not the Sluman I know," I defended.

Sluman scored 74-73 over the first thirty-six holes to make the cut. At the start of the third round, his caddie arrived at the first tee before Jeff. He spotted a pink ribbon on my blazer, and he asked why I was wearing it. I told him my wife was battling breast cancer.

"Don't tell Jeff," I instructed. We made a deal. I was aware of Linda Sluman's medical expertise. I did not want to burden the Slumans.

Jeff was battling to add the U.S. Open to a major championship résumé that included a victory at the 1988 PGA Championship.

In Round Three, Jeff improved his position with a two-over-par 72. He was now solidly in contention to win the U.S. Open.

On Sunday, I wished Jeff a happy Father's Day. He returned the sentiment. Then he looked at me and asked, "How's your wife?" I knew Jeff's caddie had shared our secret.

"She's doing OK, thank you," I said. "Now go win the U.S. Open."

"Ladies and gentlemen . . . from Hinsdale, Illinois . . . Jeff Sluman," I announced moments later. I joined the crowd in applause. His drive was in the fairway's center. He marched off.

He got as far down the fairway as I hit a wedge, then turned. He headed toward me.

"What have I done now?" I wondered. It couldn't have been the intro. Hinsdale and Jeff Sluman are easy.

He had a serious look, the one I'd seen before his start. He took out a piece of paper and wrote his cell phone number.

"Call me," he said. "Maybe Linda can help." At that moment, the condition of my wife was more important than even the U.S. Open.

He scored 69 on Sunday to tie for the day's low round. It was karma. He deserved that and more.

Like the golf lesson he had promised a young boy, Jeff had shown concern for someone else. Selfish he is not. Selfless he is.

After flying home on Tuesday, I called the chair of the Registration Committee. She had tallied the votes of my survey. I told her what Jeff had done. Her feelings changed. She "flipped" her vote.

"I'm calling every member of the committee to tell them," she said.

She did. They had a second vote. The outcome was different. They discovered what I already knew.

46

2006: Good Things
Come in Small Packages

THEY STOOD IN UNISON. At the 2006 U.S. Open at Winged Foot, thousands in the grandstand welcomed him when he set foot on the first tee. The name of the player was well known, like Arnold, Tiger or Phil. It was Tadd Fujikawa. It was an emotional experience for all, including the first-tee starter.

The kid would probably look little Eddie Lowery in the eye. Eddie was the ten-year-old caddie for U.S. Open champion Francis Ouimet ninety-four years earlier at The Country Club in Massachusetts.

* * *

At age fifteen, Tadd was the youngest golfer to ever play in our National Championship, and though small in stature at five-foot-one, he received the biggest welcome.

First to play in Tadd's group at 8:50 A.M. on Thursday was John Koskinen of St. Petersburg, Florida. There was polite applause. Next to play was Tadd.

When I began his introduction, the gallery gave the young Hawaiian a second standing ovation. That had never before happened in my memory. It might only happen in New York. I stopped the introduction. I really had no choice. I couldn't speak. Nothing came out. I was choked by the occasion. I needed to pause. Tadd did not stop. He marched confidently to the tee. He had the demeanor of Arnold Palmer. "Charge!"

If Tadd was nervous, it didn't show. He drove about 285 yards, slowed only by the right rough. He shot 81, followed by 77 on Friday. He could be proud in that he finished ahead of former major champions Mark Calcavecchia and Nick Price.

No, Tadd Fukikawa did not make the cut. He made only friends, all the way from New York City to Honolulu. He still does.

47

2000: Jeff Coston at Pebble Beach

A TEACHING PROFESSIONAL WANTED TO GIVE HIS CHILDHOOD DREAM ONE MORE TRY. Why not? This one was not just another U.S. Open. It was the centennial of the National Championship. It would be the beginning of the new millennium, and it would be played at Pebble Beach. What's not to like about this scenario?

The player was Jeff Coston.

Jeff had already proved he could play big-time golf. He qualified as an amateur for the 1977 Open at Southern Hills and again in 1978 at Cherry Hills, his first year as a pro.

But something else made this attempt even more special. His son, Tyler, would be his caddie if he made it to Pebble Beach.

Team Coston had one more hurdle before Pebble Beach. It was Sectional Qualifying at Pumpkin Ridge Golf Club, near Portland, Oregon.

For Tyler, nineteen, the walk was the easy part. He was a basketball star at Portland State. For Jeff, forty-four, it was a marathon. The format definitely favored youths, not middle-aged golfers, especially those making a living standing all day on a lesson tee. Jeff taught at the Semiahmoo Resort in Washington, near the Canadian border. They hoped the day would end happily at sunset without having to endure a playoff.

We met on the first tee on a cool, drizzly Oregon morning. They hoped the day would be one to long remember, but a day not too long.

"After you sent us off . . . I was teary-eyed, really," Jeff recalled, " . . . thinking of the dreams I'd had of this day . . . playing in the Open . . . the goals I'd had . . . and the failures along the way. I knew I had to get control of myself." He did early in the round.

Jeff scored 70 in the morning round. With another solid round, he had a good chance, but scores were bunched and a playoff after the second round seemed likely. That, Jeff did not need.

Though weary, Jeff held on in the afternoon. He posted another 70 for a total of 140, two under par on the Ghost Creek Course. The wait was agonizing until all scores were posted.

As darkness approached, I watched the Costons sitting near the scoring table. Their body language left me in doubt as to how they viewed their chances.

Are they grieving or celebrating? I couldn't tell. They showed plenty of emotion. I did not wish to intrude.

A moment later, they were smiling. Only then was it clear. Jeff had just qualified for the 100th U.S. Open.

"What am I going to do?" Jeff asked Tyler. "I have a hundred students coming from Japan next Monday!" Monday was not to be any Monday. It was the first day of U.S. Open week.

Would he forgo a dream because of his business commitment? The answer quickly became obvious. He would attempt to reschedule his students. He hoped they could change travel plans on short notice.

When the tears dried, I asked, "Jeff, how do you like being . . . the last player . . . gaining a spot in the 100th United States Open at Pebble Beach?"

"You're kidding me!" he said. "The last?"

The results from the Oregon Sectional completed the field. Jeff was, indeed, the 156th player to qualify. Only Tag Riddings had bettered his score. Both would advance to Pebble Beach if Jeff could change his teaching commitment.

I left them in celebration and to work out the details of his conflict. I hoped to see them the following week.

I introduced Jeff all four rounds. With scores of 70-77, he made the cut. A third-round 80 found the Blaine, Washington, resident paired with Colin Montgomerie in the final round. Monty had come close to winning several U.S. Opens, including 1992 at Pebble Beach.

When Jeff and Colin arrived early on the first tee, I greeted them as I did others: "Happy Father's Day." Something very special followed.

"When I saw you at Pumpkin Ridge," I asked Jeff, "did you ever think you would be playing with Colin Montgomerie . . . on Father's Day . . . at the 100th U.S. Open . . . with your son on the bag?"

"Never," Coston said. It was an emotion-filled moment for a father, his son, and me.

More than nine thousand others who had tried to qualify would have traded almost anything for the dream Jeff had made come true.

"Before the start that Sunday," Jeff told me, "I said to Tyler, 'I need to know, Son, am I still your hero?' "

The answer did not come until later that Father's Day. Colin had posted 73; Jeff had 74. With an embrace in the scorer's tent, Tyler finally answered his father's question.

"Dad," said Tyler. "You'll always be my hero."

48

Nicklaus at Registration

"IF YOU DON'T HAVE SOMETHING NICE TO SAY, DON'T SAY IT AT ALL." Mom must have said that to me a hundred times—maybe more.

Jack Nicklaus is the greatest golfer of the last half millennium, about the time the Scots invented the game. This coincides with Christopher Columbus setting foot in America.

Columbus's discovery was his greatest achievement. What Jack attained in golf, I contend, was not his greatest accomplishment.

Put aside all his successes—eighteen professional majors—plus two U.S. Amateur titles, the design of more than fifty-seven courses worldwide and his vast other business ventures.

Jack's No. 1 feat, in my view, is the rearing of five terrific children with Barbara. Added to all that are twenty-two beautiful grandchildren.

Make no mistake. Barbara has been as great a champion at home as Jack has been on the course. Together, Barbara and Jack are parents to be admired by everyone. They are among my idols.

With reverence disclosed, I share an occurrence at Player Registration at the 1999 U.S. Open at Pinehurst.

Upon arrival at the U.S. Open, a player's first step is to register in order to provide necessary information for the week—a local address, phone numbers, and other required information, like that required by the Internal Revenue Service.

We were about to close registration on Monday of Open week. A dozen volunteers and USGA staff were preparing to go home after a long day. The first players had begun to register at 7 A.M. It was a pleasant surprise when Jack wandered into registration, unexpectedly, around 6 P.M. Even though registration was officially closed, we were going to reopen.

Jack's appearance made the long day worthwhile. He was alone, without entourage, like some. He was friendly, mortal, and very much at ease.

As the committee reorganized, I welcomed Jack to this Open, as I'd done so many times previously. This occasion, though, was to be a little different. It was to be his last U.S. Open.

Jack obviously needed no introduction to this admiring group, but out of respect, I gave him an impromptu, special introduction anyway.

"Ladies and gentlemen—the greatest golfer to ever play the game."

We first met in 1972 during a practice round prior to the Open at Pebble Beach. He played with friend Bob Hoag and big Bill O'Connor, as well as my friend, Lawson Little III. I tagged along.

Growing up in the Midwest, I knew Jack's upbringing—the importance of his father, a successful pharmacist, in his life. He'd grown up at the Scioto Country Club in Columbus, Ohio, under the tutelage of professional Jack Grout. We even had a mutual friend, John Roberts, who had followed many steps in Jack's climb from being the best junior golfer ever to becoming the best golfer of all time.

In the center of the activity to reopen registration, I engaged Jack in a personal conversation. We talked briefly about our children—his five, my two.

Michael Nicklaus and our son, Ryan, were friends in their early teens, playing like kids at the Open—driving go-carts, packing their clubs at Southampton Golf Club, even getting into some mischief. Michael once broke a window at their rental house near Shinnecock, somehow managing to—unintentionally—hit a sand wedge backward! Ten minutes after the accident, Ryan, Michael, and his dad were all kids, playing a game—stacking quarters on their elbows, then seeing how many they could catch before the coins hit the kitchen floor. Coins were everywhere!

But the broken window was now long forgiven. As we waited, Jack bragged about

Jack, Jr. Jackie had passed the Local Qualifying test in Florida, advancing in a playoff. Unfortunately, he was not successful at the second stage, Sectional Qualifying. Otherwise, his namesake would have joined Dad in his "last" Open.

*　*　*

Our friendly conversation then turned to the business at hand. Registration was ready for Jack. The first thing he did was admire the U.S. Open trophy. Many players ignored or never looked at the trophy, as though it was a bad omen. Not Jack. He smiled, holding it and seeing his name engraved four times.

His second stop at registration was with USGA's Keith Russinoff. Keith presented an IRS form requiring a Social Security number. Jack had gone through this procedure hundreds of times over his forty-year career, but on this one occasion, he could not remember his employment number. Jack removed his wallet in search of the number. He fumbled and mumbled. I began to laugh.

"Why are you laughing?" he asked.

"Nothing," My mother's admonition had suddenly come back to me.

Jack went on, still mumbling, relating that kids, like Michael, all remembered important numbers because, today, everything is computerized.

I chuckled at this sight and sound.

"Why are you laughing?" he again asked.

"Nothing!" I resisted sharing my inner thoughts of his fortunate childhood.

Now clearly frustrated, Jack had his wallet out, and he began to spread its belongings. Credit cards were everywhere. His Social Security card remained in hiding.

I had done my best, but I could not contain my laughter at this rare sight. With all his successes, the Man was human!

"Why are you laughing?" This time, he added a glare.

It was the third time Jack had asked. I could no longer contain myself.

"Why should you remember your Social Security number?" I asked. "Have you ever had a job?"

I immediately wished for a retraction.

The silence of prayer followed for what seemed the time Jack stood over a putt. Then, Jack cut the moment of tension.

"No, I never have had a job," he blurted.

The group erupted in laughter, including Jack. It was good fun. Once again, Jack proved he's so much more than our game's greatest champion.

This story circulated. At a dinner, USGA president Trey Holland chided, with tongue firmly planted in cheek, that I might get my résumé updated—and to know my Social Security number because I would soon be looking for a job!

I apologize for breaking Mom's rule.

49

Jack Nicklaus: The Softer Side

A S OPINED EARLIER, CHAMPIONSHIP GOLF CAN BE A SELF-CENTERED ENDEAVOR. It's an individual effort, requiring long hours of practice, followed by intense competition. There's extensive travel and, often, countless days away from family.

Greatness only comes from sacrifice and total dedication. Jack Nicklaus had all of that, but he had more. He also had Barbara Nicklaus closely at his side.

Jack had a focus of few, which helped him attain the status of, in my opinion, "Greatest Golfer since the Fifteenth Century." Winning was everything. Only Hogan, Tiger, Tom Watson, Bernhard Langer, and perhaps Vijay Singh may have matched Jack's devotion to being the best over a long period—more than forty years. Others have tried, though their years of success were far shorter.

Jack was the toughest of competitors. However, he had a soft side. It wasn't always seen or shared in his most competitive years. I was lucky in that I often saw a softer Nicklaus. My experience was sometimes from the distance of a gimme putt.

My first remembrance of seeing Jack came in 1968. I was a private in the army. I volunteered to be a gallery marshal at the Bing Crosby National Pro-Am at Pebble Beach. During a heavy rain delay, I was in the small locker room next to Pebble's pro shop, and there he was — the Golden Bear with his caddie, Dede Gonzalez. I didn't dare say a word.

Jack and Dede went through many boxes of golf hats. The issue seemed silly. It was the color of the bands on those hats. Jack selected a hat with a band that he thought matched his shirt and slacks. DeDe rejected the combination. Back and forth they went, going through countless combinations, trying to find a match. I'm not sure they ever agreed. Later, I learned Jack is colorblind. Thankfully, he has Barbara to dress him, too.

After leaving the army, I joined the Northern California Golf Association staff. Our headquarters were above the ninth green at Spyglass Hill, which allowed me to watch many friendly, practice round matches during the Crosby.

Jack often paired with longtime friends Bob Hogue or Pandel Savic to take on Arnold Palmer and Mark McCormack. Arnold would tease Jack, who was facing a tricky four-foot putt, "Jack, if you *think* you can make it, it's good." Later in the match, Jack might return the favor. When the match got to the eighteenth hole, there were no concessions. "Putt it" was heard. They were very good, but competitive, friends.

Over the next few years, I got to know the Nicklaus family. I was often in Jack's gallery with Barbara, who walked every step with her husband. She carried a small box. In it was Woodstock, the little bird of Peanuts fame. When Jack made a birdie, Barbara would wind the toy and the little bird would celebrate in the small box.

There wasn't much celebrating in Jack's fourth round of the 1976 Crosby. Rolling out new clubs, he shot 82—10 over par—at Pebble Beach. I sent him a photo from the disappointing round. He was smiling in the picture. He signed it, "Sure doesn't look like a guy shooting 82."

The following July, the PGA Championship was at Pebble Beach. Jackie, fifteen, was going to attempt to qualify for the U.S. Amateur the next day at nearby Almaden Country Club. I took him there for a practice round. On the eighteenth hole, he narrowly missed a double eagle, tapping in for an eagle, his first ever. I was more excited than he was. Jackie's dad missed winning the PGA by one stroke. The following day, Jackie missed qualifying for the Amateur, but ever since, he's been known as "Eagle" to me.

50

1994: Joey Ferrari—The Biggest Smile at the U.S. Open

ADOUBLE-BOGEY FINISH ON THE LAST HOLE OFTEN LEAVES A GOLFER DISCONSOLATE, especially when a berth in the U.S. Open is at stake.

Not Joey Ferrari.

After signing his scorecard at Congressional Country Club, in Bethesda, Maryland, he learned he had qualified for the 1994 U.S. Open at Oakmont and an ever-present smile grew even longer.

When he arrived at Oakmont a week later, his smile stretched from his home in Stockton, California, to Western Pennsylvania.

Joey played in the Northern California Junior Championship in the 1970s, when I was charged with conducting it. He never won, but you would never know it. His happiness was contagious to all.

Over the years, Joey was successful in amateur golf on a national level. He was runner-up to Jeff Thomas in the 1993 U.S. Mid-Amateur Championship at Eugene Country Club in Oregon. Even in defeat, his demeanor was that of the winner. Something happened in that match that said a great deal about Joey Ferrari.

On the 31st hole of the match, Joey was 2 down with six holes to play. It appeared he would go 3 down with just five holes to play after he drove poorly, and his ball came to rest near a tree. As he contemplated a strategy, an unusual thing happened.

The match's referee made a sudden announcement to the hushed crowd of perhaps a thousand:

"Ladies and gentlemen, immediately on completion of the match, we will have an awards presentation."

Hearing that, Joey looked up and smiled.

"Uh, this match isn't over yet," he announced to all. It was a light-hearted moment that broke the tension of the match.

Joey managed halves on the 31st and 32nd holes before losing the 33rd. Now 3 down, it appeared the match might indeed end soon. Perhaps inspired by the referee's proclamation, he won the 34th and 35th holes.

Hold that trophy presentation!

Joey's comeback ended when a 10-foot birdie putt hit the back of the hole but refused to fall. Thomas won,1 up. You wouldn't know it by the look on Ferrari's face.

When Joey arrived at Player Registration at Oakmont nine months later, the two of us beamed. It was a special moment.

"Do I have a surprise for you!" I said, leading him to the sheet where players signed up for practice rounds.

Two players had already signed up for a round on Wednesday morning. They were Arnold and Jack. Need I say more?

"Joey, the sign-up is a democratic process here," I opined. "Arnold played a practice round at Olympic in 1955 with Rod Curl, an unknown, and a Wintu Indian from Redding (California). They became friends. Why don't you join Arnie and Jack?"

He froze but smiled.

"Sign me up," he said.

The sheet read: Palmer, Nicklaus, Ferrari.

It clearly illustrated the fairness of the U.S. Open. Everyone was equal. They would be golfers. Together, they'd won twenty-five majors.

Joey had two days to think about playing with the legends. He thought about how Jack and Arnie had squared off thirty-two years earlier at Oakmont in a playoff for the U.S. Open title.

When he arrived on the first tee, early Wednesday, Tom Watson was just heading off as a single player. There were also fifteen thousand others awaiting Arnold and Jack.

"When they arrived, my legs went numb," Joey recalled. "I suddenly couldn't think of a swing thought. It dawned on me I might kill somebody if I hooked my tee shot. Heck, I might even whiff it. Those were the wild thoughts going through my mind. It was way too much."

"Jack," he said, "if it's OK, I'm going to just drop one down there and play with Tom."

"OK," Jack said. Arnold laughed.

Off Joey scampered to the fairway, joining Watson. The two played a more relaxed practice round.

Joey Ferrari was player No. 156, the last player to start in Round One.

He missed the cut, but you would not have known it. His smile and memories have lasted forever.

51

Arnold Palmer:
The Goodness of the Man

T O MANY, THE MAN WAS BIGGER THAN LIFE, BUT HE WAS NEVER LARGER THAN THE SPORT HE LOVED.

He knew his place in golf and life, and he brought everyone around him on his magical journey—even me—on countless occasions. Arnold Palmer had no greater quality, making his legion of admirers feel so much a part of what he felt inside the ropes.

Arnold and I were not intimately close. It took me almost forty years to stop calling him Mr. Palmer, but he was never "Arnie." That was reserved for his closest of friends. In some ways, though, I may have known him like those much closer. That was Arnold's nature.

My first remembrance was late 1977.

Bing Crosby had died. The future of his "Crosby Clambake" was in doubt. I was working at the Northern California Golf Association. Among my duties was organizing a banquet for the California Golf Writers Association. Given the questionable state of the tournament, I convinced my boss, Bob Hanna, that we should hold the CGWA dinner on Tuesday evening of the Pro-Am. I reached out first to Arnold. He immediately said "Yes" and the success of our first CWGA banquet at Pebble Beach was all but assured. Little did I know what would follow.

Tom Watson also would attend. Now feeling rather ebullient, I contacted Barbara Nicklaus. She delivered her husband.

Jack, Arnold, and Tom were all going to participate out of their respect for Bing, the father of golf's first pro-am.

We weren't finished yet! I had targeted one more to make the foursome.

A close friend called to say, "You've got him; Bob Hope will attend."

It was golf's "Four Eagles"—Hope, Nicklaus, Watson, and Palmer, and it all started with Arnold's acceptance. Where Arnold went, others followed. Ask those at The Open Championship.

Even Arnold's arrival that evening was special. He slipped in a side door at Monterey Peninsula Country Club. He was clad in a tartan jacket, looking princely. He spotted my secretary, Sue Land, greeting guests. He slid onto the piano bench next to her. Sue looked over and almost passed out. She was not the only lady to do so.

By 1982, the CGWA event was enormously successful, and I had moved on to the USGA. I was assigned to the Senior Open at Portland Golf Club.

The defending champion was Arnold Palmer. Event chairman Elon Ellis knew the marketing power of Arnold, and so he strung a banner over Scholls Ferry Road, near the club. It read: "Arnie's Coming." The Senior Open was an enormous success.

Corporate involvement in golf was in an early stage. There were only three hospitality tents, and one of those was sponsored by Lanier, the office copier company. Every day, Arnold, its celebrated spokesman, visited their tent to greet guests. One lady actually fainted in Arnold's arms.

The Senior Open starter (me) was nervous. I had done some starting at the Crosby, but this was the Senior Open! I was so clueless that I didn't recognize some of the legendary golfers. I actually asked the great Peter Thomson his name when he arrived on the tee to play with Arnold. Twenty-two years later at St. Andrews, I apologized to Peter, a five-time Open champion.

On Sunday of that Senior Open, eventual champion Miller Barber and Arnold were paired. The pairing sheet read: Arnold D. Palmer, Ligonier, Pennsylvania. What came out of my mouth was "Lanier, Pennsylvania." Before playing, Arnold came over and whispered, "I hope you got paid very well to say that."

I introduced Arnold from the first tee on many other occasions and never again made that mistake.

My most memorable intro of the great man was in 1994 at Oakmont Country Club. It was his last U.S. Open.

As Rocco Mediate and John Mahaffey waited, Arnold had yet to appear on the tee. We knew where he was by the crowd's buzz. We were getting close to the start, so I dispatched security guards to assist him. With seconds to spare, Arnold came through the crowd. His caddie, Royce, was nowhere to be seen, and Arnold had only his putter.

First to play was Rocco. After his introduction, Rocco teed his ball left, then picked it up and teed a second time to the right. I knew immediately that Rocco was stalling. Royce was still missing. Then, it was Mahaffey's turn. He followed Rocco's example.

At last, Royce appeared. He'd apparently been tossing clubs along the way to get to the maximum number—fourteen. My introduction went perfectly. Arnold wagged the driver, then stopped.

"Clyde, please count my clubs." Referee Clyde Luther counted. Arnold counted. Royce counted. I even joined the huddle in counting. Finally, we all got the correct number—thirteen, plus the driver Arnold held.

Off they went, finally. I breathed a sigh.

Before that group was scheduled to play on Friday, I did something defying all logic. I taped a copy of Decision 6-3/3 to the starter's table. That Decision stated that all players had to be on the tee at one time, ready to play. Those words were highlighted in yellow.

Why Arnold Palmer, playing his final round in the U.S. Open, warranted a lecture on lateness from me, could only be deemed as zany.

Well, the King arrived early. I weighed his state of mind. It was good. It was always good. I directed him to the Decision. He read it and smiled, remembering that he only had his putter on Thursday.

Then, always quick of wit, he said, "If you'd have introduced me, I'd have used my putter. I'd have hit it from here to there, to the ladies' tee.

I was with Arnold several times at St. Andrews, but I'll only share a story from his visit in 2004, the 250th anniversary of the Royal & Ancient Golf Club of St. Andrews.

I was scheduled to play Kingsbarns Golf Course on the same day that Arnold, club captain the Duke of York, PGA Tour Commissioner Tim Finchem, and club secretary Sir Michael Bonnalack were to play a quiet, unpublicized round there. Preferring to watch this celebrated match, I offered my spot to Trip Kuehne, the great amateur golfer and a three-time Walker Cup team member. I then bounced back and forth between both groups.

After fourteen holes, Trip Kuehne was 7 under par. I raced back to the eleventh hole to share the news with Arnold, who knew Trip. Together, we walked a long distance to the twelfth tee. It was not an easy walk for the seventy-five-year-old.

"Gents," Arnold told his distinguished group before the long walk, "I'll be right back."

Putting everything else aside, together we hiked a long way to the fifteenth hole. Trip, naturally, had the honor and was ready to play. Ward Johnson and Pete Ridder were intently watching the possibility of course-record history, but now they turned to see Arnold Palmer.

"I hear you're playing pretty good," Arnold said. The three golfers could not have been more surprised by their gracious guest.

Kuehne finished 7 under and established the amateur record there, too.

I could go on about Arnold's goodness but will end with one very personal bit of advice he gave me.

We had been having a drink with a mutual friend, Dr. Tom Loss, at the U.S. Open at Oakland Hills in 1996.

When we were alone, I asked, "How are you doing?"

He had shared that he had prostate cancer. He didn't tell the world until October. Then he admonished, "Get your PSA. Get your PSA."

I did, regularly. Twelve years later, his advice saved my life.

In golf, Arnold was arguably the game's brightest star. In life, he was an entire galaxy.

52

I Have a Dream, Too

THE 1993 U.S. SENIOR OPEN WAS PROCEEDING NORMALLY, WITHOUT INCIDENT OR FAN-FARE.

Then, out of the blue, a spectator leaned over the ropes at the first tee and tapped me on the shoulder. Surprised, I turned.

"See that fellow; he's not a competitor," he said. He pointed to a man putting on the green below the first tee. I was thunderstruck by the accusation. There were a couple of reasons. How could a noncompetitor be on the practice green?

"Which one?" I asked.

"Yes, that man," he said.

He pointed to a gentleman stroking short putts.

I was busy sending out players, but it seemed appropriate to take a moment to check. I raced down the hill, having little time to formulate a proper plan for approaching the man.

"Excuse me," I said. The tall gent turned. "Are you a competitor?"

My bluntness rocked him. The answer was clear. His players' badge was on his belt.

"Bill Wright," it read.

"Yes, I am."

Embarrassed, I apologized and scurried back up the hill to find the accuser. The guy was gone. I ducked under the ropes and went on a quick search, but to no avail. I was hot, sensing what the man's real motive might have been. I cringe to this day.

Moments later, Bill Wright came to the tee. My anger showed. Again, I apologized. I tried to hide my feeling with the introduction.

"Ladies and gentlemen, please welcome the 1959 United States Amateur Public Links champion . . . from Los Angeles . . . Bill Wright."

Given the circumstance, I wanted Bill to select a driver and smash it 340 yards on the green, as Arnie had done at the 1960 U.S. Open. Instead, he drew a five-iron from the bag.

"A good play," I thought, but I was wrong.

Bill struck the ball squarely on the hosel—a dreaded shank. It went far right, over the crowd, into the ninth fairway. It was not any player's desired start. Off he went, shoulders already drooping, in pursuit of the errant shot. Bill's wife was easily picked out in the crowd. Her head was lowered, too. He did, however, manage a respectable bogey 5 on his opening hole.

With an evening to think of how to make amends, I had an idea. I went to Tom Meeks to explain. We agreed to invite Bill to be our special guest and to speak at the U.S. Public Links the following week at Riverdale Dunes, near Denver.

Upon arrival for Round Two, I extended our invitation, and he accepted. Moments later, his five-iron landed safely in the first fairway. Bill and wife, Ceta, smiled more broadly this time.

He missed the cut at Cherry Hills, but things went better at Riverdale Dunes. Bill's remarks were the highlight of the Players Dinner.

* * *

A few years later, our paths crossed at a function in Southern California, where Bill was introduced as the USGA's first African-American National Champion.

That was awkward, I thought to myself, to have that qualifier added to his accomplishment.

Bill showed the audience the gold medal he had won. It's the same medal given to every National Champion. His pride was mine, too.

In 2010, we met again at a dinner honoring Bill. He had grown up playing Seattle's Jefferson Park Municipal Golf Course, also the home course of Fred Couples. The dinner was at Broadmoor Golf Club. It was Bill's first visit to the prestigious downtown club. Bill and Ceta greeted me warmly. Then, I had a moment of curiosity. "Bill, where's your gold medal?"

"Ceta!" Bill exclaimed, "Show him the medal!"

She was now wearing it on a necklace. It was a special moment, but things got even better. That evening, Bill was introduced simply as a National Champion.

My dream is coming true.

53

Paul Simson — The Theft
of a Walker Cup Berth

THE AMATEUR CAREER OF PAUL SIMSON HAS FEW EQUALS, AND IT RANKS WITH ANY IN RECENT DECADES.

In senior amateur golf, he, arguably, has no equal. In 2010, at age sixty-one, he won the U.S., Canadian, and British Senior Amateur titles—a first.

The only thing missing on his résumé was his dream of competing in the Walker Cup. He focused on that dream for eight years in the 1990s. In the end, it was taken from him at the U.S. Open. I was there, nearby. That's why I took a special interest.

At age forty-seven, Simson was competing in the U.S. Open. He wanted to win, but his first goal was to make the cut. That would elevate his chances of achieving the dream.

The Walker Cup had special importance for me, too. I was involved in conducting the 1981 Match at Cypress Point Club. That one experience was the pinnacle of my forty-three years in conducting competitions, and it strengthened my advocacy for veteran career amateurs being selected for the U.S. team.

In recent years, the Walker Cup has become increasingly dominated by collegians, young golfers whose sights are set on careers as professionals. I applaud their ambition. However, many turn pro within days of the Cup, some with guaranteed endorsements in their back pockets.

That was never Paul's ambition.

On day one at The Olympic Club in 1998, he scored 76 with two triple bogeys.

One came at the tenth hole, where demons of golf struck.

There, Simson pulled his drive into the left trees on the par-4 dogleg right. During the search for the ball, referee Stuart Reid did what good officials do. He asked spectators what they had seen. It was rumored someone had run off with the ball. Stuart weighed the evidence, but he could not prove the theft. After a five-minute search, Stuart declared the ball lost. Paul returned to the tee to put another ball into play.

He could have asked to play a second ball, scored with both balls, then appealed to the committee. He chose not to do so. Thus, the result was a triple-bogey 7.

Word spread about Paul's incident. I learned of it when Bob Callan approached me. My friend shared startling news. He knew what happened to Paul's ball. Bob's daughter and a friend witnessed a young man pick up Paul's ball, then disappear.

What now? The matter was over. Paul's score was posted. There was no erasure. As Tom Meeks, a longtime USGA staff member in the Rules and Competitions Department, once said, "Hard luck has to start someplace."

With the disappearance of the ball, the clock of bad luck had begun for Paul, and its first tick was on the tenth hole.

* * *

The U.S. Open is a very busy place. It's often difficult to communicate with others on a timely basis, either by phone or radio. I wasn't sure what to do with the credible evidence Bob shared. I surmised that when members of the media learned what really happened, the USGA might not be viewed favorably. With Bob's help, I gathered his daughter and friend. We audio-taped their story. We now had an accurate account. I tried, unsuccessfully, to reach the boss, David Fay, executive director of the USGA.

David finally called back. He was unhappy, perhaps tired from explaining a slippery hole location on the eighteenth green. He was taking it out on me!

"I understand you have a video of what happened to Simson's ball?"

"Not so," I responded. "We have an audio tape from two ladies who saw the incident. I knew the press would be all over it. I taped their story—only trying to protect the USGA."

It was a short conversation. Eighteen-hour days at the Open do that.

The second day, Simson scored a respectable 72. His 148 total was one stroke above the cut.

Paul's lifetime dream disappeared with the theft of his ball. He wasn't the first to leave his heart in San Francisco.

54

1998: Matt Kuchar Was Steamed

MATT KUCHAR WAS AMATEUR GOLF'S BRIGHTEST STAR, AND THERE WAS TALK HE MIGHT DO SOMETHING HIGHLY UNUSUAL. Like another Georgia Tech grad, Bobby Jones, it was rumored Matt might remain an amateur golfer.

Both had won the biggest play-for-fun prize—the U.S. Amateur.

When Matt arrived at The Olympic Club, he learned he would play in the traditional grouping that featured the U.S. Amateur champion with the current U.S. and British Open winners. That alone would have been a lifetime thrill, but there was a bonus. Matt's father, Peter, would be his caddie. Dad had also caddied in the Masters in April.

At Augusta, several players noted that Peter was sometimes exuberant in support of his son, and several made their feelings politely known.

On Friday at Olympic, Justin Leonard had a bit of a dust-up with Peter after Matt chipped in during the second round. They resolved it in a gentlemanly manner. In the end, Matt tied for fourteenth, eight strokes behind winner Lee Janzen. Matt's star grew even brighter.

With Matt's success came instant celebrity.

David Letterman wasted no time. Letterman sent word to The Olympic Club that he would like Matt to appear on his late-night TV show. Matt's expenses would be paid to New York. The question was whether the payment of expenses violated the Rules of Amateur Status, something the USGA guarded dearly in those days.

Would the USGA permit Matt to accept first-class air and Waldorf-Astoria accommodations? The Letterman executives wanted an answer.

Matt was not even aware of the invitation.

Immediately upon the Open's conclusion, an impromptu meeting was held. The USGA Amateur Status Committee huddled. The setting was unusual—in the middle of a party, the U.S. Open's Toast to the Champion, and on the dance floor at Olympic. They considered Letterman's invitation. Chairman Fred Ridley, now chairman of the Masters, presided.

They voted approval. Matt could accept expenses money to appear on Letterman's show.

Matt still didn't know about the invitation. I was asked to tell him. That order proved easier given than accomplished.

The Olympic Club may be bigger than the White House, and I had little clue as to where to find Kuchar. The final round was over, and most players have no reason to hang around after the finish.

While Matt is very close to his dad, Peter, I was told he was seeking some private time after the hectic week.

Off I went in pursuit of Matt. A half-hour into my search, the trail was still cold. Little did I know that was about to change, literally.

His locker was still intact with clothes hung. So I knew he was still on the premises, but where?

Then, I got a bright idea: Ask the head locker attendant because they know everything.

"I think he's in the steam bath," the attendant said. Luckily, I'd been there once myself. Only this time, I was fully clothed. Now, dressed in USGA blazer and bowtie, I popped the door open and entered. The fog was denser than San Francisco's famous covering. I could see nothing.

"Matt, are you in here?" There was urgency in my voice.

"Yeah, I'm over here!" he responded. I could not see him. He was more fortunate than me. Matt was probably in his birthday best; I was wearing a jacket and tie. Today, this seems a funny visual.

I explained the Letterman invitation and the USGA's approval. Then, I raced back to the party, dripping, but parched. Mission accomplished.

55

1990: There's a First Time for Everything

W E WERE ABOUT TO MAKE U.S. OPEN HISTORY. If Hale Irwin parred the eighteenth hole and Mike Donald made a bogey, there would be a sudden-death playoff. In eighty-nine previous U.S. Opens, there had never been one to determine the national champion.

Donald and Irwin tied at 280, 8 under par after seventy-two holes, necessitating the eighteen-hole playoff on Monday. Donald had a one-stroke lead going to the final hole. If they remained tied, the playoff would continue, hole by hole, until a champion was determined.

The rules were clear. The problem was that the USGA had never faced this situation. Frankly, we weren't prepared. Confusion was imminent.

As Donald prepared to putt for a par and the title, C. Grant Spaeth, then the president of the USGA who was refereeing the playoff, called me. He, too, suddenly realized the playoff might go beyond eighteen holes.

"Read, do we have a flagstick in on No. 1?" There was panic in Grant's voice in his radio transmission.

I sprinted in full USGA jacket-and-tie attire from the eighteenth green to the first tee. I was happy to see there were tee markers. I didn't stop there. I continued down the first fairway. When I got to the apex of the dogleg, I radioed back to Grant. There was good news and bad.

"Grant, the flagstick was just put in on No. 1, but not on No. 2."

If the extra-hole playoff went more than one hole, certainly it wouldn't look good that the players might walk onto the tee, glance at the green and see no flagstick. There was a narrow bridge over the lake to the No. 2 green, slowing its access. Thankfully, Superintendent Chris Hague anticipated the problem and was already in motion, locating flagsticks.

There were other things to worry about first. I ran back to the first tee. Hale parred. Mike narrowly missed his putt for par and the title. The playoff continued.

A stampede was headed my way at No. 1. Thousands rushed to the first tee. They lined the fairway. Gallery marshals who worked the hole when the playoff began had left their posts and most had joined the gallery. Some returned to assist. The scene had the look and organization of the field after a football game. People were everywhere.

Fortunately, my starter's box with the necessary materials was in the Medinah starter's hut. I hand-scribbled the names of the two players on scorecards. The players arrived with Spaeth and P. J. Boatwright Jr. The continuance of their play was only a few minutes away. I gave the scorecards to the players.

Spaeth instructed Irwin to play away first. Both players drove it into the fairway, then each hit the green. Hale sank a 12-foot putt for a birdie to secure his third U.S. Open title. Thousands surrounding the green saw the conclusion. So did millions on ABC.

Mike signed Hale's scorecard and handed it to me. Not giving it much thought, I put the card in my blazer pocket.

We held the traditional Toast to the Champion in the Medinah clubhouse, where volunteers shared a little time with Hale before he was hustled to the media center for interviews. He happily spent an hour there.

After his time with the press, Mike disappeared.

Two hours later, Ray Anderson, a member of the USGA Executive Committee, and I were reliving the historic day in the clubhouse. Everybody had gone home. Or so we thought.

Suddenly there was a banging on the door. As first, we ignored it. It continued. We went to the door. It was none other than Mike Donald.

Actually, Mike was not alone. His mother and caddie were nearby. They had been sitting outside on a bench, having a few beers.

Then, Mike shocked us.

"Why did Hale play first?" Mike asked.

Ray and I looked at each other. We were stumped and speechless.

The order of play in most playoffs is determined by lot—drawing straws or tossing a coin. Since Hale had the lower score at the eighteenth hole, Spaeth simply decided Hale should play first, as he would in match play. In the rush to start, we forgot official protocol.

Mike persisted in a gentlemanly manner. We didn't have a good answer. Finally, we told Mike he was right, but we offered advice.

"Mike, it's over," I said. "Nothing's going to change the outcome."

The next day, we read about our conversation with Mike in the *Chicago Sun-Times*. A journalist nearby heard all, and he reported the error.

That wasn't our only faux pas.

A month later, my blazer came back from the dry cleaner. Pinned to it was Hale Irwin's scorecard. I had forgotten about putting it there after Mike had signed it. I stared in disbelief. It bore the signature of only its scorer—Mike Donald. Hale Irwin had not signed it. It was technical error. The world knew that Hale had won his third U.S. Open.

I decided to have some fun.

Six months later, we honored Irwin at the California Golf Writers Dinner, held annually during the Bing Crosby National Pro-Am. I brought him to the microphone with this introduction: "Hale, you think you won the U.S. Open, but we have proof otherwise. Here's your scorecard with only one signature—that of Mike Donald!"

In college, Hale had been a defensive back at University of Colorado, and he could still run. He grabbed the scorecard in the blink of an eye and added his signature.

Yes, a Committee occasionally makes mistakes. However, the Committee's decision is final and is never wrong.

56

1997: Faldo: I Wouldn't Want to Play in the Tiger Circus Again

NOT EVERYONE HAS SEEN A SOFT SIDE OF NICK FALDO. I have. Readers can go elsewhere to read about the sometime-petulant nature of England's greatest golfer.

I first saw Nick's goodness at the 1993 U.S. Open. I gave him a ride to his hotel after a Saturday practice round at Baltusrol. Our conversation centered on his once-in-a-lifetime meeting with Ben Hogan that spring. The purpose was to learn how to win the U.S. Open. Faldo was obsessed. He was 0-for-6 at that point in his career. Hogan was one of four players to win it four times.

Nick eagerly traveled to meet Hogan. He had several legal pad pages of questions, but he never got to ask most of them. Nick said Ben shared openly. It was a meeting of two very private, and perhaps misunderstood, champions.

Interestingly, their meeting did not help. Nick finished seventy-second at Baltusrol, his lowest finish in eighteen U.S. Open attempts.

Four years later, Nick was again within striking distance in the Open at Congressional Country Club. The final-round pairing was Faldo and rising star Tiger Woods, the first time they'd ever been in the same pairing. Tiger scored 72 to finish twentieth; Faldo's 76 gave him a share of forty-eighth.

After that round, something very personal happened.

I was in the lower parking lot that was reserved for players. Nick's caddie, Fanny Sunneson, was headed my way. Nick trailed her. He looked like the Pied Piper, followed by a long string of kids seeking autographs. Fanny approached me to say he wanted to speak. Suddenly, the kids disappeared, leaving us alone between all the courtesy cars. There I was, one-on-one, again, with a superstar.

He shared that he and Tiger had been "put on the clock" for slow play. He explained his side of the story. They had, indeed, fallen behind. He blamed the large gallery and the entourage of writers and photographers who followed. In his view, he and Tiger were blameless. Though Nick was known as a very deliberate player, I was empathetic.

It was a very emotional moment with Nick Faldo. He might express it differently today. "I wouldn't want to play in the Tiger circus again."

That was June 15, 1997.

Well, they did meet again. Nick drew Tiger in the first round at the World Match Play in 1999. Given Nick's comment in the parking lot, the outcome of their match was no surprise. Tiger won, 4 and 3. Had I known the pairing, I'd have placed a bet.

Later that summer, Nick was over the loss. We shared a laugh during a practice round before the U.S. Open at Olympic Club, where this time he finished forty-eighth. The visit with Hogan never resulted in the dream Nick so badly sought.

57

Where'd All These
People Come From?

P LAYERS HAVE WIDELY DIFFERENT VIEWS ABOUT BEING CAUGHT UP IN THE ADDED AT-
TENTION THAT TIGER WOODS BRINGS TO AN EVENT, especially one with greater importance, like the U.S. Open.

Some enjoy being paired with Woods, believing it helps them concentrate because
there are larger crowds following a Woods pairing, television cameras are never far
away, and players want to do well under the spotlight. Others dislike the experience,
even being in the group in front or behind Woods because of the higher number of
people following that group. When Tiger holes out, so many fans and writers head to
the next hole that it's often distracting to players who still need to putt out.

Jeff Wilson of Fairfield, California, is a player who's seen both sides of the coin. A
former runner-up in the California Amateur, he's won the U.S. Senior Amateur and
became only the second player to be low amateur at a U.S. Open and a U.S. Senior
Open.

As one of California's top amateurs over the last twenty-five years or so, he's
managed to play in four U.S. Opens, two in his home state: in 2000 at Pebble Beach
and 2008 at Torrey Pines.

At Pebble Beach, he remembers, "I went out for my Monday practice round at
3:30 P.M. by myself. There were a few people mingling around the pro shop and a few
volunteer marshals down each side of the first fairway and around the first green.
There were very few spectators.

"At the time, the Casa Palmero (a Mediterranean-inspired estate) was still under construction, and they had a staging area to the right of the second teeing ground. As I was about to tee off at the second hole, up from the hedges—out of nowhere—came Mark O'Meara, Hank Haney, Butch Harmon, and Tiger. I was no longer a single. The next four holes were crazy with people running across fairways, up from the beach; it was like a scene from *Caddyshack*.

"By the time we got to the fifth hole, the stands were full, and the hole was lined with spectators. In a way, it was really uncomfortable, but it very much helped me on the first tee Thursday. Tiger could not have been nicer. He went out of his way to make me feel comfortable. He took pictures with my family; it was a great memory, and I've always been a Tiger fan."

In 2008 at Torrey Pines, that was the U.S. Open in which the USGA departed from its customary defending-champion pairing.

On Thursday and Friday that week, Wilson was paired with Brett Quigley and Freddie Jacobson, and they went off two groups in front of Tiger, Phil Mickelson, and Adam Scott.

"You do your best and try to calm yourself before you get to the first tee," Wilson says, "but then I walked through the tunnel, under the grandstands, and saw the stands full. The fairway was lined all the way to the green and there had to be a half a dozen cameras all pointed at the small teeing ground. At that moment, I remember being extremely nervous—I mean, like, hard-to-breathe nervous."

Wilson shot 78-80 the first two days and says the most significant factor was emotional.

"For those two days," he said, "I definitely felt overwhelmed, and it's really difficult to get it back at that point. I hit so many really poor shots those two days it was almost unbelievable.

"I parted the stands on the fifteenth with a skull out of the bunker. I had to drop from a hot dog stand and got a standing ovation for making an 8-foot putt for triple bogey. I got to the sixteenth tee and was apologizing to my playing partners. Brett said, 'That's the loudest ovation we've had in two days.'

"Sometimes when you lose it, there is no coming back. It wasn't my finest golf, but there are some funny memories."

58

1991: Jack: I'm Never Going to Hit Another Bad Shot

M Y FEELINGS ABOUT THE 1991 U.S. OPEN WERE MIXED. My mother had passed away the previous week after a long illness. She especially wanted to be at this Open. She had never attended one to see her son start the U.S. Open.

I thought about skipping that week at Hazeltine National Golf Club, just west of Minneapolis, Minnesota. In the end, there was no choice. My mother would have wanted it no other way. She and her seven brothers and sisters had lost their mother early in their lives. So, siblings did what good families do. They look after each other. They were tough, too. In many ways, I was like the family's ninth child. I had to carry on.

My knowledge of Minnesota golf was zero. I recalled the criticism the club endured at the 1970 U.S. Open. Professional Dave Hill said architect Robert Trent Jones Sr. had ruined a good cornfield with his design! My parking spot for that week was in that cornfield, far from the clubhouse.

On the drive to the golf course on the Friday before the Open, I drove past the home of a singer named Prince. I had never heard of him, but I imagined he had to be very successful to live in a purple house. The man had quite a spread!

While spinning the radio dial, I began to understand how big this Open in Minnesota was going to be. It seemed every station was already broadcasting from Hazeltine, and the Open was still a week away.

"If you don't have tickets, get out here today," I heard over my car radio. "This is your last chance to see this great course and to get your logoed Open merchandise."

This was new, even for the Open. Thousands must have been listening. When I finally arrived at Hazeltine, they directed me to that cornfield. I parked next to golf-crazed Minnesotans who had shopping bags full of shirts and caps. Others were racing to get theirs. This would be a special week, and it proved so. Minnesota broke previous attendance records, and it was the first sold-out U.S. Open.

It was good that I went. Mom was there, too. She didn't need a seat. She was in my thoughts and on my shoulder.

* * *

There were a couple of pairings that stood out that week. One of them was Open champions Jerry Pate and Andy North in a group with Jack Nicklaus.

Jack was hurting with a bad back. His first tee shot showed it. He yanked it short left. Jerry Pate described it as going about forty yards. He limped after the ball, finding it in the rough.

"If that son-of-a-gun makes par from there," said Pate recalled, "I'm walking in."

Jack hacked a nine-iron back into the fairway, then a two-iron from 220 yards to 15 feet. His par putt barely missed. Pate shook his head and continued play.

Jack somehow managed a 2-under-par 70, bettering North by one and Pate by eight. He was three strokes behind co-leaders Payne Stewart and Nolan Henke. I commended him later, but he added, "That's the worst tee shot I've seen."

My words could have been chosen more diplomatically. Perhaps it was my blunt German heritage, like Jack's. He looked at me not just like The Bear, but a grizzly bear.

Round 2 was different. He smashed this drive down the middle. Off he went, still gimpy, looking like a fifty-year-old with a troubled back. He got to the ladies' tees, now called forward markers, turned, and headed back in my direction. Uncertain of Jack's intention, I side-stepped left. He did, too. Then, I went right. So did Jack. I felt very uneasy being pursued by this bear.

"What did I do wrong this time?" I thought to myself. Then it crossed my mind that this would be payback for my earlier rude remark.

"Did you notice the difference?" he asked.

Dumbfounded, I said, "No. The caddies and scorers were in front of me. I couldn't see you. . . . Only the result."

"My stance!" Jack said. "Pate told me . . . after the round . . . my stance was too narrow. . . . I guess I did that because of my back."

Jack had emphasized Jerry's advice had come after the round. He knew the rules, and advice during play was prohibited.

"I widened my stance today."

Then, he astounded me with what he said next: "I'm never going to hit another bad shot!"

Imagine: The greatest golfer of all time was telling a weak six-handicap that, like all golfers, he'd "found it."

Now, Jack Nicklaus left me shaking my head. Again.

59

Janzen: Failing at Cleanup Duty

T HE TEMPERATURES—ONE HUNDRED DEGREES OR CLOSE TO IT, WITH HUMIDITY TO MATCH—WERE NOT THE ONLY THINGS HOT IN TULSA.

Players were, too. This was the U.S. Open, where the relationship between players and USGA is often cholla-like.

Mistakes at the Open become magnified, both by players and the media. Occasional slip-ups are to be expected, but this one had the potential to rank among the most infamous, among them the unmown fairways in 1976 at Atlanta Athletic Club, an order to take down a plane over Oakmont in 1983, an unfortunate hole location in 1998 at The Olympic Club, the Dustin Johnson situation at Oakmont in 2016, and controversies at Shinnecock Hills in 2004 and 2018.

This unforced error at Southern Hills in 2001, however, was a new gaffe.

A mistake was made in the pairings for the third round. It was the result of a late penalty assessed on Lee Janzen.

The issue began in Thursday's first round when a thunderstorm rolled through Oklahoma, a state well known for its electrical storms and worse. Play was suspended immediately. Players marked their balls, quickly, using a tee. This suspension was an order to immediately halt play. Among those still on the course was Janzen, the Open's 1993 and 1998 champion. Everybody hustled to the safety of the clubhouse.

Janzen marked his ball in the middle of the ninth fairway, then sprinted to the clubhouse.

When the round resumed Friday morning, Janzen noticed something unusual. He looked around and noticed all areas on the fairway had been dried with squeegees in order to remove excess water. For some reason, the area around his ball had been skipped. The maintenance staff avoided it, probably not wanting to disturb the tee Janzen had left to mark the position of his ball. After deliberating, Janzen took action into his own hands.

He used a towel to dry the area around his ball. Ironically, he was probably entitled to relief from casual water—had he asked the rules official walking with his group. He finished Round One Friday morning and signed his scorecard for a disappointing 77, eleven strokes behind leader Retief Goosen. He was well outside the projected cut and the prospect of a third title seemed out of reach.

Jim Halliday was the referee for Janzen's group that fateful day. Jim is a five-star expert on the rules. He observed the "mopping" on Friday from a distance, but he didn't give Janzen's action much thought at the time.

Friday night, Jim awakened from another lightning storm. Something troubled him beside the storm.

Like many rules officials, the *Decisions on* the *Rules of Golf* are never far away, and in this instance, the publication was bedside. He read (then) Rule 13-2, stating what is prohibited and permitted in the area around a player's ball. He also read all the relative cases on the rule; he wished he hadn't. It was an *oh-no* moment. The rule prohibited removal of dew or moisture from around a ball. Halliday went sleepless until sunrise. Then he beelined to the rules trailer to report the incident to the committee.

Thirty-three players had yet to finish Round Two, which had been pushed back until Saturday morning. Janzen was among those, unaware the committee was deliberating his action from the day before. It was a difficult decision.

Janzen had violated Rule 13-2, but he did not know it when he signed his scorecard. The committee eventually decided, fairly, to waive golf's version of the death penalty—disqualification—for having signed an incorrect scorecard. To do otherwise would have been unfair. How could the rules penalize him certifying his score when he didn't know he had violated Rule 13-2?

However, the committee decided it could not excuse his violation of Rule 13-2. His toweling the area was a violation. The committee imposed a penalty of two strokes. The penalty strokes were added to his first-round 77, making it a 79. All this took place without Janzen's knowledge. Nobody else knew, either.

On Saturday, Lee played like a guy trying, first, to make the cut, then to win his third Open. He was grinding, not knowing the committee was deciding his future at Southern Hills. He birdied his thirty-sixth hole to post 68, a remarkable comeback. It was one of the better scores in mostly rainy, windy conditions. His total of 145 appeared to be one stroke inside the 146 cutline. He had accomplished his goal—so he thought. He had no idea of the drama taking place behind the scenes.

Neither did Kevin O'Connor. His job—scoring—was one of the important jobs at the Open. Accuracy is imperative. There is zero tolerance for any scoring error by players or the committee. Once scores were certified, O'Connor made the pairings for Round Three.

The Janzen issue was doubly complicated by shortness of time. NBC waited. Players waited. Spectators waited. The USGA had a tiny window—less than an hour—for starting Round Three. That was the time from the last putt being holed in Round Two until the start of Round Three.

While Kevin checked and rechecked the scores, eighty players had made the cut, including Janzen. Having finished a quick lunch, Lee was preparing for Round Three.

The first tee was a busy place. Players milled, wanting to know their starting times. Media folks pressed for answers, too. Everybody was still "in the dark" on this bright, sunny day. NBC's Roger Maltbie paced, ready to accompany a featured group onto the course.

* * *

Voila! There was Kevin. He had raced from the scoring trailer to the first tee. He was breathless. He handed me pairings, starting times and a deck of freshly printed scorecards. Word on any problems still had not reached either of us. Like Sgt. Schultz on *Hogan's Heroes*, we knew nothing.

I announced the early pairings to the crowd, which was growing exponentially.

I handed out scorecards to the first group. There was an urgency to get started so the third round could be completed by Saturday evening.

As quickly as Kevin had appeared, everything came to a halt. We had a big problem. It was not as bad as a tornado twisting toward Tulsa, but this one left a few of us swirling.

Word came by radio that Janzen had been penalized. The two-stroke penalty caused him to miss the cut. It also meant the early pairings had to be corrected. Now there were seventy-nine players playing the final two rounds—not eighty. In disbelief, Kevin sprinted back to his trailer to undo all his good work, then redo it.

Players were puzzled. They knew nothing about the penalty or the resultant confusion. I wanted to keep it that way. It was not yet like a prison riot, but players were not happy. It was not a situation for which I had prepared.

I went from starting Round Three to damage control within seconds. l was going to try to reorganize the U.S. Open without players, NBC, media, or spectators knowing the debacle that had developed. My goal was to keep it all a secret.

As players grumbled, I killed time.

In a poor attempt at humor, I asked the group of six or eight assembled players, "Who would you like to play with?" They didn't laugh. It was a bad joke.

Ten minutes later, O'Connor reappeared. Color had returned to his face. Corrections were made, pairings revised, and scorecards reshuffled. Nobody in the media seemed to know our secret.

* * *

I stepped to the microphone.

"Ladies and gentlemen, welcome to Round Three in the 101st United States Open Championship . . ."

It was not my happiest start. We were missing one of Open history's brightest stars.

However, we had avoided disaster, and nobody seemed to know. Kevin and I certainly did.

Shortly before the start, Janzen received the unfortunate word by phone. He was hurt, understandably, but he took the decision like the gentleman he is.

"All I wanted was a chance on the weekend," he said, "but I've learned, once it's over, it's over. In golf, you move on."

Lee Janzen was a great U.S. Open champion, but he was a better man in my mind.

60

2001: A Scout's Motto: 'Be Prepared'

RADIOS—SOME MIGHT CALL THEM WALKIE-TALKIES—WERE INTRODUCED TO GOLF IN THE EARLY 1980S.

Among their advantages, they enabled officials to communicate easily when players found themselves in confusing rules situations.

Radios sometimes brought needed humor to the long days of conducting championship golf.

I recall several "light" radio transmissions.

On one occasion an official was asked his location, not once or twice, but three times. There was no response to the question, only silence. On the fourth attempt to reach the official, there was finally a response. It was simply the sound of a flush and rumbling water. A verbal response was not necessary.

At some Opens, transmissions were more about nongolf issues. Hours, it seemed, were spent updating scores in the India vs. England cricket match rather than on the *Rules of Golf*.

Usually, though, conversation was about the rules or how the day was proceeding from an administrative standpoint.

An unusual radio call was broadcast at Southern Hills in 2001. Notah Begay had left the first tee only minutes before rules official Stu Reid radioed an urgent request. Notah needed more golf balls—now—after playing only one hole.

The "one-ball rule" was in effect. It required players to use the same make and model of golf ball, with identical markings and characteristics, for the entire round.

"How can Notah need more golf balls after playing only one hole?" I wondered.

Notah discovered he had only one ball with the unique marking of "T.W." It was rumored that Tiger Woods, his college teammate at Stanford, was the only golfer in the world allowed to play the T.W. ball.

So how did Notah get that ball? And, more importantly at the moment, how was he going to obtain more balls identical to it?

The Tulsa club is recognized for its hills but is also known for its water hazards—sixteen of them. Notah's predicament meant that, unless he quickly found more balls with the special T.W. marking, he would be required to finish the next seventeen holes with that one T.W. ball.

Reid's SOS received immediate attention. Somehow, T.W. balls were found, not in Tiger's locker, but a sleeve of balls came from Harrison Frazar.

Notah played ultra-conservatively until T.W. balls were delivered.

There was irony in Notah's situation.

In the 2000 U.S. Open at Pebble Beach, Tiger came to the eighteenth hole with a whopping eight-stroke lead over Miguel Angel Jimenez.

At the finishing hole, Tiger pulled his drive into the Stillwater Bay, then expressed himself before NBC could hit the bleep button. Caddie Steve Williams suggested he use an iron next, from the tee, for his third stroke. Tiger rejected that notion and, again, went with the driver. He made 4 with the second ball to post 6 for the hole, giving him a six-stroke lead over Jimenez in second place.

Later, Tiger learned that his caddie had offered sound advice in suggesting a more conservative shot. The ball he put into play was the last one in his bag.

To this day, I laugh thinking two guys from prestigious Stanford should know better.

61

1983: Creative Accounting:
You Do What You Have to Do

A S THE 1983 U.S. OPEN WAS WINDING DOWN, I WAS GIVEN AN ASSIGNMENT FROM TOM MEEKS—one that had nothing to do with the Open, the game of golf, or its rules.

"Get us over Hulton Bridge, Ronny," Meeks ordered.

From the U.S. Open, about fifteen miles northeast of Pittsburgh, Pennsylvania, Tom and I were scheduled to fly to Honolulu the next day for the U.S. Women's Amateur Public Links. Anyone who's ever been to Oakmont for a major championship knows of the logistical nightmare. The course is on a two-lane road that leads across the Allegheny River, and there's no alternative except Hulton Road and Hulton Bridge in order to reach a highway to head toward Pittsburgh.

Trying to find a way to beat thirty thousand spectators and an army of U.S. Open shuttle vehicles in a race over the Allegheny River, passage was stop-and-go under the best of circumstances. After the U.S. Open, it was guaranteed gridlock for hours.

While Tom had dumped the problem on me, he did offer one creative thought—get a motorcycle-police escort. We concluded it was our only hope. We were both well motivated to succeed. First, if we didn't make the flight, we'd both be looking for *real* jobs. Second, our destination was Hawaii.

I had little time to pull it off.

We got lucky. Somehow, I found not one, but two, off-duty motorcycle policemen. I explained our plight and they thought they could provide assistance.

"Best case," one said, "the trip (to the airport) will take forty-two minutes." They gave no assurance. Payment would be upfront—three hundred dollars—in cash. I was scraping to come up with the stipend but managed to gather the funds.

The chaotic issues at Oakmont appeared to be coming to a head, including the hellacious thunderhead clouds. When the storm struck, lightning sent everybody scrambling, including our motorcycle escorts.

And when they fled, so, too, did three hundred of my "closest friends" who never were to be seen again. The officers were without blame. There was no way to find them.

Thankfully, our Plan B, a taxi, was waiting. The driver performed a miracle; he got to the airport in exactly forty-two minutes. We looked like we had swum the Allegheny.

We made the flight and arrived in Honolulu still wearing the same rain-soaked clothing from eighteen hours earlier.

I hope the statute of limitations has run out on the expense report I filed in 1983 over Oakmont.

62

2000: Jack Says
Farewell to the U.S. Open

Jack Nicklaus's retirement plan unexpectedly changed on October 25, 1999, the date of Payne Stewart's fatal flight.

Jack accepted an invitation to fill the starting position of the national champion from the previous year. 2000 would be his last U.S. Open, and the fact that the 2000 U.S. Open was played at Pebble Beach would be even more memorable.

On Tuesday, a salute to Payne was held. Forty pros participated, including Paul Azinger, David Duval, Phil Mickelson, Davis Love III, and Tom Lehman. They lined the eighteenth fairway and simultaneously hit tee shots into Stillwater Bay in a unique remembrance to the 1991 and 1999 U.S. Open champion.

Jack could not participate in the ceremony. He quietly had his own idea about paying tribute to Payne.

On our way to the ceremony, rules official Steve Foehl and I spotted Byron Nelson walking to the tribute, and we offered the octogenarian a ride, thus violating all golf cart rules. Any time with Byron was worth the reprimand.

After this special occasion, we returned the 1939 champion to the residence of Mrs. Eddie Lowery, widow of Francis Ouimet's boy caddie in the 1913 U.S. Open at The Country Club.

On Thursday, Byron was on the first tee an hour early to witness Jack Nicklaus's start. NBC's Roger Maltbie was there because he was scheduled to follow Jack's group, but before that, he had a request. For Roger, I would do almost anything.

"Wouldn't it be nice," Roger asked, "if we did something special to remember Payne when Jack plays?"

"Roger, that's a great idea," I said. "But we did that yesterday at the Salute."

Roger accepted my decision, then disappeared. It seemed the end of any further tribute.

Jack arrived on the first tee early. He, too, had a special request.

"Wouldn't it be nice if we honored Payne?" Jack asked.

Roger and the Golden Bear had clearly spoken.

"Jack, we did that yesterday," I appealed. "Folks higher than my pay grade decided to hold the Salute only."

Saying *no* to Jack Nicklaus is not easy or fun.

A second thought came to me. I asked him to join me privately.

"When you are introduced," I said, "you can do anything. I have no control. It's your stage. Just don't tell anybody we agreed on this, including the press. It's between you and me, OK?"

We had a deal.

Minutes later, Paul Lawrie was introduced, followed by David Gossett, the U.S. Amateur champion. All eyes turned to Payne's stand-in.

It was an emotional moment for everybody, including me. "Don't blow it," was my thought.

"Ladies and gentlemen"—my voice was strong—"from North . . . Palm Beach, Florida . . . the 1962 . . . 1967 . . . 1972 . . . and 1980 . . . United States Open champion—Jack Nicklaus."

Thousands applauded.

Jack paused. With voice breaking, Jack surprised everyone.

"I just want to take a moment," he said, "to remember our national champion."

There wasn't a dry eye anywhere.

Son Jackie gave Dad a towel. Jack shed a tear with all gathered, including me. Golf's greatest champion then took a moment to compose himself before he put his tee in the ground.

It was a moment few will forget.

The next day was Jack's final round in the U.S. Open.

This time was different. Jack spryly came to the tee for the 8:20 starting time. Trey Holland, then the president of the USGA, was there.

Jack looked me in the eye.

"Well, did I get you in trouble?"

The question caught me off guard. It surprised Holland, too, now puzzled, having no idea that Jack and I had made a deal. I read Trey's stare to mean, "Ron, what did you do now?"

"I told the press," Jack sheepishly confessed. "They asked me in the media center, and I told them."

We laughed. Trey understood.

63

1993: This Tiger Was Never a Kitten

THE KID WAS ALREADY A PHENOM AT AGE SEVENTEEN. He had the attention of a rock star. He was exposed to it early. At age two, he made his TV debut on *The Mike Douglas Show* with Bob Hope and Jimmy Stewart. When Tiger was four, professional Rudy Duran took Tiger under his teaching wing. At six, he won the Drive, Pitch, and Putt for kids under ten. He won San Diego's World Junior six times. The kid didn't need a trophy cabinet. He already needed a trophy house.

I had seen Tiger play several times in his youth. The first was at Pebble Beach in the California Amateur, which he never won. Later, I watched him defeat Notah Begay in the quarterfinals of the U.S. Junior Amateur at Lake Merced Golf Club in 1990. I had not yet seen the fiery competitive spirit that made him a champion. That insight came at the U.S. Open Sectional Qualifier at Valencia Golf Club.

Because of Tiger's celebrity and all of the media attention, I was asked to assist at that qualifying. The assignment seemed odd. I wondered how a seventeen-year-old high school senior could possibly deserve so much media attention. I arrived at Valencia before sunrise and immediately realized I was wrong. Media trucks were there from all over Southern California. They anticipated telling the world that Tiger Woods had advanced to his first U.S. Open at Baltusrol.

Tiger was on the cusp of fulfilling everyone's dream late in the second round. I stayed near him most of the day to assist with any rulings, but also to be of assistance to the large gathering of media folks. With a few holes to play, I was behind the green

185

when he flew an iron shot over the green. The ball bounced off a golf cart and into an awful lie. Tiger let his feelings be known about the position of the chairman's cart. While observing, I resisted asking if he considered the fact he'd chosen the wrong club. Tiger was hot. It's fair to say Earl, his dad, who was nearby, was also.

Tiger had a competitive fire and it was blazing.

Tiger was not successful at Valencia. His bogey after the misfortune left him one stroke over the score needed to qualify. Adding to his frustration was one lad who did advance. It was Ted Oh, sixteen, who earned the spot in the Open. Ted was one of Tiger's biggest rivals in Southern California junior golf.

I guided Ted through Player Registration a week later at Baltusrol, then led him to his locker. Because lockers generally are assigned in alphabetical order, his was between Jack Nicklaus and Mark O'Meara. It was a special moment for the youngster, seeing the company he had joined.

To date, it's been Ted's only appearance in the U.S. Open. When it mattered most to both, Ted beat Tiger Woods to gain that once-in-a-lifetime experience for most.

Tiger rebounded nicely from that disappointing day at Valencia. Seven years later, he won his first U.S. Open at Pebble Beach, beating the world's best by fifteen strokes. Since then, he hasn't stopped roaring.

64

2006: 'Build It Day One to Hold the U.S. Open': The Story of Chambers Bay

O N ORDERS FROM PRESIDENT THOMAS JEFFERSON, LEWIS AND CLARK DISCOVERED THE POTENTIAL OF THE PACIFIC NORTHWEST. Their expedition took the explorers two years.

Orders were never issued for my expedition. As a normal part of representing the USGA in the West, I simply went looking. My goal was to present to the USGA a course with the potential to host the U.S. Open. What I found in the land of Lewis and Clark was a golf epiphany.

I embarked on this journey knowing two things. First, the Northwest had never hosted the National Championship and, second, the region and its golf legions deserved the Open after 115 years.

Mine was a long trip. It took twenty-three years. Looking back, it would have been nice to have been paid by the hour!

In reflecting on the journey, I traced its origin to one event—the 1982 U.S. Senior Open at Portland Golf Club. This championship opened my eyes to golf in the Northwest, and it energized me to find an Open site.

I knew the course had to be exceptional, of the caliber of the many in the East, like Shinnecock Hills, Winged Foot, Pinehurst, The Country Club, Bethpage Black, or Oakmont, as well as Pebble Beach in the West. Those sites are on the Open's regular rotation.

My journey was circuitous. It took me to eight courses—all new. There was no preference of one state over the other—Washington or Oregon. Golfers in both have a love and a passion for the game, play actively, rain or shine, and are tradition-minded. If a U.S. Open were finally held there, fans would come in record numbers, just as they did in the 1982 Senior Open.

After 1982, I asked myself, "Why hasn't the Northwest ever held the U.S. Open?"

Let me make one thing clear. I was not the decision maker in selecting Chambers Bay. Others did, and they did so in less than two years after my visit to the site. My role was in identifying a rare site that met all requirements. Chambers Bay did. There was never a doubt. The course would challenge the world's best, and the property was huge, as big as any previous Open site.

My backseat role was happily accepted. The selection of Chambers Bay will always be a source of pride.

In telling this, my focus, first, is on the whirlwind final three years, 2005-08.

The most valuable player of this story was John Ladenburg, executive officer of Pierce County.

John was a visionary. He saw the potential of a 930-acre sand quarry. He envisioned a golf course that would attract golfers locally and from around the globe, much like St. Andrews, Pinehurst, Pebble Beach, or Bandon Dunes.

John's childhood may have prepared him for the battle that followed. He was one of sixteen children. He learned at an early age that things didn't always go his way, but he also learned to never give up. The ups and downs of golf taught him that, too. In the end, his leadership won a very tough match.

In September 2005, John convinced county officials, by a 4-3 vote, to spend $25 million of public funds to build a course that turned out to be Chambers Bay. That decision was not universally popular. Pierce County, the state's largest, had plenty of golf—public and private. Citizens asked about the need for another, especially one financed and owned by the public.

After that vote, the County considered more than four dozen golf course architects. That might be a record. Candidate John Harbottle Jr. was the odds-on-favorite. Tacoma bred, he was an outstanding young architect, and he was the eldest son of a celebrated golf family—Pat and Dr. John Harbottle Sr. Pat had won a USGA championship as a teen and John Sr. contended in several U.S. Senior Amateurs. Their son would have been a sound and popular choice.

Against formidable competition, the design team of Robert Trent Jones Jr. also came from a famous golf family. His father, Robert Trent Jones Sr., had more than 350 courses to his credit, including famous U.S. Open venues such as Oakland Hills and Baltusrol. His brother, Rees, added more than 225 more. Together, they had designed and renovated more courses that hosted Opens than any other architect.

Bob Jr. designed 275 courses worldwide, but none had been selected for the U.S. Open. Chambers Bay would be Bob's legacy. That was a significant motivating factor. I knew it, though we never talked about it.

* * *

Bob and his senior partner, Bruce Charlton, introduced me to the project at a Christmas party in 2005. After plying me with eggnog, they gleefully described a sand quarry south of Tacoma. I had heard about the site and about the politics John Ladenburg had weathered. They asked me to visit Chambers Bay soon thereafter.

This would be my eighth visit to a Pacific Northwest site I hoped could host the National Championship.

Shortly after the party, I joined Ladenburg and Jones on the rim of Chambers Bay. I rendered a verdict within minutes.

"We build it, Day One, to hold the U.S. Open." Those were my first words after taking in the spectacular sights.

John and I had just met. Only then did I learn that we shared the same dream.

Bob's goals were already clear. He and his design team deserved to join his family in U.S. Open history.

Now others had to see it.

After our morning tour, I called Mike Davis at the USGA.

"You've got to see this! It can handle the Open," I excitedly reported.

Mike and I had worked well together on many occasions—U.S. Opens since 1991, U.S. Amateurs, Mid-Amateurs, a Senior Amateur, a Senior Open, and one U.S. Junior. We had played plenty of golf, and he had mocked my swing and persimmon-headed driver in places such as Bermuda, Scotland, and Pebble Beach.

We shared a passion for golf played on the ground—true links golf.

We were the USGA's pioneers at Bandon Dunes in 1997. We returned to its dunes regularly during construction and then for the opening in 1999. We visited Bandon so often that USGA executive director David Fay decreed, "No more!" He was tired of hearing about Bandon. Later, David surrendered. Bandon was on the radar of golfers everywhere, as well as the USGA.

Bandon Dunes didn't need an advertising budget. I was it. They labeled me their "Bell Cow."

"Build it and they'll come" was never more appropriate. Golfers came. The USGA came, too, with the Curtis Cup, plus five other national championships. The 2020 U.S. Amateur is next.

Davis and I were on the same page about sites suitable for national championships. He was receptive to my report about Chambers Bay. He scheduled a visit to Tacoma. When his entourage arrived, I knew the USGA was serious. The group included Fay, agronomist Larry Gilhuly, Jim Hyler of the Executive Committee, and Davis. They joined Ladenburg, Jones, Charlton, and Read.

The ball was rolling.

David Fay's attendance was particularly meaningful. First, I viewed David as a skeptic. More importantly, it was David's vision that made the 2002 U.S. Open at Bethpage State Park on Long Island a reality. He did so after receiving a tip from Jay Mottola of the Metropolitan Golf Association. Taking the national championship to a municipal course was risky, and it was a monumental change in USGA thinking. David took a big chance, and his political skills, much like Ladenburg's, opened minds and doors at other municipalities. The success of 2002 proved the U.S. Open could be played on other long-overlooked but great public courses.

The Open at Bethpage had added importance. It was enormously important to New York City. It was the area's "coming out" after 9/11. Yes, Tiger won, but chants of "Rudy, Rudy, Rudy . . . " were heard everywhere. Mayor Rudy Giuliani was bigger than Tiger.

David's bold decision, along with the USGA's investment in Bethpage, was a defining moment in U.S. Open history. It changed the thinking about where the Open could be played. Fay's message was clear. Public golf mattered. Torrey Pines, near San Diego, California, came next in 2008. Many of us doubled our efforts to find new Open venues.

My best candidate was already identified.

After the USGA's visit to Chambers Bay in 2006, my role ended. Others did the heavy lifting. My visits were infrequent, only to gawk and to smile at Jones's progress.

My focus turned elsewhere. I identified sites for Senior Opens that went to Sahalee in 2010 (east of Seattle, Washington), and Del Paso Country Club (Sacramento, California) in 2015, and for the Women's Open in 2016 at Corde Valle (south of San Jose, California), another Jones design.

In the meantime, the USGA and Pierce County were negotiating through 2007. Jones and I knew little about the behind-the-scenes discussions quietly being conducted.

That changed at 7 A.M. on February 9, 2008, only two years after visiting Chambers Bay. The USGA stunned the world of golf. It announced the 2010 U.S. Amateur, followed by the 2015 U.S. Open at Chambers Bay.

With the announcement, Chambers Bay earned two blue ribbons. It would be the first Open site in 115 years in the Northwest, and it was the first course built with one goal—to host our National Championship. One other, Minnesota's Hazeltine National Golf Club, dreamed an Open might someday be in its future. Chambers Bay targeted the Open on Day One. In less than ten years after construction began, it succeeded.

Bob Jones learned of the USGA's decision on Friday, the day before the official announcement. On Saturday night, we celebrated.

Bob, Eddie Merrins, Dave Potus, and I enjoyed dinner sporadically. We kept telling Jones, "Get off the phone." Congratulations came from around the world. Bob deserved the recognition, and he was finally joining his father and brother in Open history. I was almost as happy as he was.

* * *

The first Northwest candidate for the Open was obvious—Portland Golf Club. PGC had already earned a monumental place in history. It and a generous member, Robert

191

Hudson, resurrected the Ryder Cup in 1947. The course was a gem, traditional and challenging, especially on its greens that could challenge those at Oakmont in difficulty. Unfortunately, PGC lacked the length required today.

Other clubs were deserving candidates. Tacoma Country & Golf Club, Waverley Country Club, and Seattle Golf Club had welcomed USGA championships at every opportunity. However, they, too, lacked the length or infrastructure required.

Sahalee Country Club was a strong candidate. Its biggest drawback was the dense evergreen forests lining fairways. This limited spectator numbers and hindered their viewing. Sahalee made changes later, thinning out about a thousand trees, leaving two thousand, enabling it to host the 1998 PGA Championship and the 2010 U.S. Senior Open, where record crowds watched Northwest natives Fred Couples and Peter Jacobsen. Once again, this proved the region would support a U.S. Open.

I kept looking. In 1989, Peter Jacobsen shared his dream—to lure the U.S. Open to his beloved Oregon. A meeting was facilitated with P. J. Boatwright Jr., who shared a checklist for Open sites. Peter ticked every box in building Oregon Golf Club to P. J.'s specifications.

In 1990, I toured OGC with Peter. Peter's SUV had its capacity of five Jacobsens and one Read, and we got stuck in a rain-soaked fairway. No problem. Peter had something, then new—a cell phone. Peter called a towing service.

"Come to fairway 1 at Oregon Golf Club," he said.

The driver did not believe Peter's instructions. GPS didn't exist. We sat for hours, sinking. When the driver finally found us, he got stuck, too. Eventually, we managed to extricate ourselves from the mess.

If I were OGC's designer, I would have left all those tire ruts as a unique design feature with no free relief. It would have served as a reminder that golf is not always fair.

Peter auditioned OGC in 1992, hosting "Peter's Party." He attracted golf's top stars, including pal Arnold Palmer. OGC never followed to pursue the Open. I kept looking.

Next came Pumpkin Ridge, west of Portland. Owners Gay Davis and Marv French cornered me late one Friday evening. I wanted to sleep. They wanted to talk.

They used magical words, "We want to build a course to hold the U.S. Open."

Rest could wait. We talked for hours. That sleepless night led to five USGA Championships, including the Women's Open and the U.S. Amateur, where Tiger ended his amateur career as champion.

Other visits included Crosswater Golf Club in Bend, Oregon, Washington National Golf Club, The Reserve near Portland, and Newcastle, a Fred Couples design that overlooks Seattle. All were excellent, but their invitations to USGA never came.

* * *

In the spring of 1997, a red-faced young man approached me in Anaheim. It was David McLay Kidd. His name wasn't familiar, but his thick Scottish brogue was.

"Miisssttterrrrr, Rrrrrread," he said. "I'm building a golf courrrse on the best golf properrrty in the worrrld."

The accent gave David credibility. He knew golf. Two weeks later, Jim Gibbons, executive director of the Oregon Golf Association, accompanied me to the Oregon coast. We were blown away—literally and figuratively. We roamed wind-blown dunes and Scottish gorse with the young architect, then in the process of building his first course. David was right in his assessment of the property. Its four courses, today, (soon to be five) are nearing "bingo" in hosting national championships. The U.S. Amateur is next, and Bandon Dunes will someday host our Open.

Chambers Bay was last.

What made it so special to me?

First was its size—more than nine hundred acres. Robert Trent Jones Jr. would have a giant sandbox on which to play. His team could route an exceptional course—priority No. 1—in any direction it chose. After determining the course's exact location, there was enormous room for infrastructure—bleachers, practice areas, a media center and television compound, hospitality, concessions, and parking. It could, indeed, be built for one reason—to hold the U.S. Open.

Chambers Bay reminded me of Royal Dornoch and Cruden Bay in Scotland with their tall sand hills. Jones could introduce a dimension often lacking in American golf—the ground game. I knew that would interest Davis.

The site had something not found in links golf—five hundred feet in elevation change. Chambers Bay and Augusta National are among the few great courses having significant elevation change of any kind.

The cement monuments, called "holding bins" on No. 18, were visually captivating. They reminded me of the cement barriers off the coast of Scotland, erected to halt a German invasion by sea in World War II. The bins were pieces of art, I thought, and they had to remain in the design. Thankfully, Jones and Ladenburg agreed.

As we talked, trains rumbled along the Bay's shoreline. The sight and sound were like Prestwick Golf Club, host of the first British Open in 1860. We talked about trains bringing spectators from Seattle and Tacoma, just as they served Prestwick and U.S. Opens at Shinnecock Hills and Olympia Fields. Train service did not happen in 2015.

I envisioned grandstands along the entire rim above the course. It would have the look of the Indy 500 straightaway with its 100,000 "cheap seats," all with unobstructed views of the entire course. This giant grandstand proved to be my fantasy.

Chambers Bay was a picture postcard in every direction. Ferry boats and pleasure crafts crisscrossed the Bay. The snow-capped Olympic Mountains were to the west, and Mount Rainier was to the east. Trains chugged along the shoreline. Autos crossed the beautiful Narrows Bridge to the north. Air traffic travelled south from Sea-Tac Airport to the north. Hikers walked and dogs played.

It reminded me of the Old Course at St. Andrews on a Sunday—a happy and beautiful place.

Everybody—golfers, spectators, and TV viewers—would be treated to an unmatched experience. Pebble Beach had stiff competition.

Weather in June would be perfect. Washington's rainy winters give way to summer sun. The Open's Thursday start and Sunday final round would be guaranteed. Weather interruptions were improbable.

Lastly, there was the intangible—the designer. For more than forty years, I have witnessed the passion Robert Trent Jones Jr. gives to his designs. His devotion today is the same as his first job in 1958, when his dad assigned him to shape the first green on Wilmington Country Club's South Course. Forty-eight years later, there was only one difference at Chambers Bay. This would be Bob's legacy. I knew what this project meant to him.

After that meeting early in 2006, John, Bob, and I left thinking the same thing: Chambers Bay would be built to hold the U.S. Open.

And, we did. Jordan Spieth won. Dustin Johnson finished second.

How can the Open not come again?

65

1983: Ping!

WHEN PETER OOSTERHUIS APPROACHED ME AT OAKMONT DURING THE 1983 U.S. OPEN, LITTLE DID I KNOW IT WOULD END UP IN A SEVEN-YEAR LEGAL BATTLE.

"What are you going to do about these clubs?" he asked.

The clubs—Ping Eye 2 irons—were his. I had no idea why the genteel Englishman was asking.

He handed me a Titleist ball. The ball looked new, and its surface was balata. Expert players preferred the balata for its softness, giving them the ability to spin the ball and make it stop quickly.

The ball was scuffed, but the cover was not cut, like it would be if I struck it in the "belly." The parallel slices were more like scrapes made if one took a knife and scratched the paint.

Peter shared his experience. He said the combination of the new Ping Eye 2 irons—with "square grooves"—meeting the soft balata ball created increased spin, even from wet grass or from tall rough. This was a new phenomenon. With traditional V-shaped grooves on irons, players were accustomed to uncontrollable shots, or flyers, from wet rough.

The reason for the increased spin, and scraped balls, he said, was the grooves. They were the futuristic irons designed by Karsten Solheim's team at Ping.

"This is not my expertise," I told him. I knew my limits. "But I'll discuss it with Mr. Boatwright."

P. J. Boatwright Jr. was recognized as the highest authority on the *Rules of Golf* and standards governing the game's equipment.

The issue was new to golf.

When we had a rain delay during Friday's second round, P. J. asked me to arrange a meeting with Peter. They were joined by others, including USGA's technical director, Frank Thomas.

I popped into the meeting periodically, realized I understood very little on the technical side, then I attended to other matters. From my brief stays, it was clear Peter was a purist and had raised the issue out of genuine concern for the impact of the square grooves on the game. He also wanted to know if he should keep playing the Ping Eye 2s.

The USGA later decreed the grooves did not conform to the *Rules of Golf.* The issue was the width of the grooves, not their square shape. Simply put, the governing body measured the width between grooves one way. Karsten Solheim, the innovative engineering genius, measured another way. When the titans could not agree, Karsten sued the USGA.

I attended meetings in rooms full of lawyers, both from the USGA and the Royal & Ancient Golf Club of St. Andrews, over the next seven years. Together, the two organizations govern the rules around the world.

Each organization had a slightly different perspective. If Ping prevailed, the USGA and R&A's ability to govern would be rocked. Also, substantial sums of money were at stake. In the case of the R&A, the individual members would be liable for treble damages. The latter was particularly troubling to the Scotland-based organization and members.

My only other direct involvement in the issue was in 1988 at the Nabisco Tour Championship at Pebble Beach.

Frank Thomas was asked to devise a study involving Tour golfers. Each would hit actual shots using wedges and seven-irons from both rough and fairway lies. Frank asked me to recruit several golfers to participate. Among those who kindly agreed were Jodie Mudd, Chip Beck, Tom Kite, Mike Reid, Curtis Strange, and Payne Stewart. They hit balls all day on the Dunes Course at Monterey Peninsula Country Club. At the conclusion, Payne went last, then stayed to socialize with the volunteers who endured a cold, blustery day.

During the study, players were never told the groove configuration of the clubs they hit—traditional V's or Ping's "square" grooves. The amount of roll from fairway and rough was measured. There was a difference favoring Ping's square grooves. Balls landed and stopped quicker.

Players like predictability. The difference in stopping was several feet.

* * *

PGA Tour Commissioner Deane Beman observed Tour players in the study for about an hour on that long day. I was told he appeared unconvinced by the data and his mind was made up. The study was a Shakespearean experience, "Much Ado about Nothing."

In 1989, reason finally prevailed as the parties settled out of court. Karsten agreed to the USGA's measuring procedure. The USGA agreed to grandfather Ping Eye 2s forever. Karsten also agreed to eventually stop manufacturing the Eye 2s.

For me, it was actually the second time to be involved in an equipment issue.

The first was during a holiday in the 1970s. I was officiating a pro-am on Hawaii's Island of Kauai. Again, it was during a rain delay.

Friend John Lotz, a former touring pro, tossed a golf ball to me. It was called a Polara. He asked if I could see a difference in this versus any other ball. In a brief inspection, I found nothing.

I handed the ball to my wife, Missy, a non-golfer. In a nanosecond, she announced, "The dimples are bigger at the equator."

John smiled. I was shocked. On closer look, Missy had been right.

John shared that the Polara would correct its curve in flight. If hooking or slicing, the ball would straighten. Again, I am no expert on equipment, but I opined that the USGA would never approve a ball with this feature. In the end, the ball was not approved, and Polara sued.

The USGA backed off to avoid antitrust laws. The ball died its own death in the marketplace. Why? It would not travel as far as the (then) new one-piece "hard" balls.

If there's one thing I learned from so many years in the game, it's that the folks who make golf clubs and balls are rather ingenious. Who knows what's next?

66

2004: My Father's Day Idea

I t WAS FATHER'S DAY. CAN THERE BE A BETTER DAY FOR A FATHER AND SON TO PLAY GOLF? So I thought.

At the 2004 U.S. Open, Jay Haas and his son, Bill, both made the cut at Shinnecock Hills. Each was at 216, six over par, after three rounds.

The pairing system software sees things in black and white. It has no flexibility—or heart. When players are tied, it pairs in the order of their finish from the most recent round. Even though the father and son were tied, the system did not pair Jay and Bill together on Sunday.

But it was Father's Day! Couldn't the computer be overruled?

I appealed to the Committee, asking for an exception. Media would love it. Jay and Bill—two of the nicest gentlemen in golf—would relish it forever. It seemed just the right thing to do. I made the case.

The Committee didn't buy it. My idea did not receive much support. The vote was Committee 1, Ron 0. Jay and Bill would not play together, even on Father's Day. Jay knew I had tried.

When Jay arrived at the first tee, Bill was already on the course. Like any father, Dad wanted to know how his son was playing. Jay was receiving updates on Bill's play. He attentively watched the scoreboard. He was also receiving text messages.

When it was time for Jay to play, he looked at me, then pointed to his watch. We were thinking the same thing. He wanted to wait, if only for a moment, to get another update on Bill's score on the second hole. Nothing was said. I got it.

What members of the Committee did not know would not hurt them, right? I delayed Jay's start. He left the tee about a minute late.

This is my *mea culpa* about Jay and Bill, but it is reported without apology. I had a heart. I'm a dad, too, and it was Father's Day.

67

It's About Time

MY MOTHER TAUGHT ME AN IMPORTANT LESSON WHEN I WAS FIVE. It was a lesson that served me well. I learned to tell time.

Time became very important in my life. While I was tardy for a few classes at Drake University, I was seldom late for anything else.

I missed a flight to Denver once, the result of a faux pas. When I parked at Monterey Airport, I looked down at my feet to see one brown shoe and one black. I had dressed in the dark.

I vowed never again to mismatch shoes or to be late.

That promise was kept at the U.S. Open. We always started on time.

Time, the exact time, is critical in championship golf. It is required for rules officials, TV, and players to all be on time.

For players, the rules stipulate a golfer must start at, but not before, one's designated starting time. Lateness is more than five minutes after one's starting time. Five minutes means five minutes—and not one second more. That one second more results in golf's death penalty—disqualification.

The exact time is important in other rules. Starting in 2019, a ball lost if not found or identified in three minutes. Precision is mandatory.

So, where do you find the exact time? I asked myself that in 1981 at the U.S. Amateur at The Olympic Club. I was first-tee starter. Someone said radio stations were the best source. I called several. Their "exact time" varied by more than a minute from station to station. That would not do. What was next?

The U.S. Navy came to the rescue. The U.S. Navy Observatory Master Clock is the country's official time. I called the phone number in Washington, D.C.

A pleasant, recorded voice gave me the time to the precise second. That same robot never knew that he was the official time at more than a hundred national championships, including twenty-three U.S. Opens.

I called the U.S.N.O.M.C. an hour before every start. Then, ten minutes before the first time, I radioed the official time to all rules officials, who set their watches to the exact second. I repeated the countdown one minute before play.

"10, 9, 8 . . . 3, 2, 1. It is now 6:59—one minute 'til game time."

This ritual occurred every morning. Some viewed me as the official time at all national championships.

At one Senior Open, Tom Meeks, championship director, radioed to me.

"Ronny, please give all officials the time."

There was silence.

"Ron Read, come in. Give the Committee the time."

More silence.

"Ron Read, please give the Committee the time." There was more urgency in his voice.

Mike Davis broke the silence.

"Tom, Ron's not here this week."

"Then call him and get the time," Meeks demanded.

It was nice to feel needed.

68

1986: My First Autograph

"WEREN'T YOU THE STARTER AT THE U.S. OPEN?"

I was flabbergasted. Barry Krueger was sitting at Dulles Airport. He approached me and my family and posed the question.

In all the years, few have ever recognized me. Then Barry asked for my autograph! That was a first. Ron Read, a guy with a modest introduction to golf, was being asked for his signature. I was incredulous.

We chatted briefly. I learned Barry was a 1982 grad from Wake Forest.

"Barry," I said. "Anybody who wants *my* autograph, then I want *his* autograph."

We each signed each other's cap. Today, I can't find my 1986 Shinnecock Hills Hogan cap with Barry's signature. That hurts. His name was always indelibly ingrained in my memory. I actually tracked him with kind assistance of his alma mater. We chatted by phone. He's a software engineer, living in Colorado Springs.

Someday, we'll play golf, hopefully at the Home of Golf—St. Andrews.

69

No Respect for the Rules

THE READ FAMILY LIVED ON RONDA ROAD IN PEBBLE BEACH, CALIFORNIA FOR TWENTY-FIVE YEARS.

Our home was known to some as USGA West. From my small office, my duties were broad, but mostly they consisted of the maintaining of relationships with state and regional golf associations in thirteen states—from Alaska to Hawaii to Texas.

Thankfully, the region was eventually downsized to ten states as more directors were added.

When I was not on an airplane, my lunch hour was often spent jogging the roads and paths of the Del Monte Forest. This routine was more than daily exercise in a beautiful setting. It was my personal relaxation—usually.

It was several miles to first pick up mail at the post office, then I'd go past the Lodge at Pebble Beach to the tennis courts at the Beach Club. Soon thereafter, I finally got to see golf being played at the second and third holes at Pebble Beach.

On one bright, sunny day, four golfers were milling about on the third tee. It didn't appear anyone had driven from the tee.

At the same time, I looked down to see a well-used golf ball sitting next to the road.

"Who'd want that ball?" I thought as I jogged along.

The ball looked like it had been through hundreds of rounds—dirty and discolored and scuffed. It certainly appeared abandoned and, after all, any player who shelled out a few hundred dollars to play Pebble Beach doesn't play a ball looking like this one did.

Weighing the inaction on the third tee, I did the unthinkable. I picked up the ball, expecting that it would go into my shag bag at home. I continued running toward the tee with the ball in hand.

As I approached the group standing on the third tee, one player suddenly turned and acknowledged me. "*Did you pick up that ball?*" he screamed.

Shocked, I responded, "Why, yes, I did."

The guy must have double bogeyed the first two holes. His lifetime experience of playing Pebble Beach was not yet realized. He was not in a good mood.

"Why did you do that?!" he bellowed.

I was so taken aback by his reaction. "I really don't know," was all I could muster.

"You are an a......!" he screamed.

He may have been right, but I felt the need to defend myself and the rules.

Nothing about my appearance or sweaty running clothes indicated I knew anything about golf.

"Look, I'm not going back to where the ball was lying," I defended. "So, first, under (old) Rule 18-1, when an outside agent (me) picks up your ball, the ball must be replaced."

They were shocked and uttered nothing. The looks of all four said everything, "Uh, who is this nerd?"

"Now," as my impromptu Rules clinic continued, "I'm not going back there to replace the ball for you. So you, under (old) Rule 20-3c(1), must drop the ball approximately where it was."

"If the road interferes," I continued (old). "Rule 24 applies, and you get one club-length from the nearest point of relief."

"Lastly, under Rule 20-2"—now I was really on a roll—stand erect, extend your arm, and drop from shoulder height."

If looks could kill, my memorial service would have started right about then. Four mouths dropped.

Finally, my primary accuser closed our encounter. "You really are an a......," he said.

I handed him the ball, then proudly headed up the hill, toward the sixteenth tee and then Crespi Lane.

Oh, how I'd love to hear how the players in that group have told the tale of their round at Pebble Beach.

70

Think the Game Has Changed?

KNOWING WILLIAM C. "BILL" CAMPBELL WAS A PRIVILEGE. Our relationship stretched from playing golf in St. Andrews and at his club in Florida to sitting on a bus bench, talking about amateur golf and the Walker Cup. I visited him at his home at the Greenbrier in West Virginia less than a year before his death in August 2013. Early on, Bill expressed that golf was the one constant in his life. He smiled in saying that.

Our pedigrees were quite different. Bill grew up at the Guyan Golf & Country Club in West Virginia. I used hand-me-down clubs to hit old balls in my neighbor's field. He attended Princeton and later won thirty-two amateur championships, including the U.S., British, and Canadian national amateur titles. I attended Drake University in Iowa's heartland, served in the U.S. Army, then won the fifth flight of my club at the Pacific Grove Municipal Golf Course.

Bill was a president of the USGA and later Captain of the Royal & Ancient Golf Club of St. Andrews, one of three Americans ever so honored. I was a staffer at the Northern California Golf Association and later the USGA.

Yes, our backgrounds were dissimilar, but it did not matter. We both loved golf, especially the amateur game.

Our dispositions were different, too. I get rather passionate in my beliefs, especially about golf. Bill was always the consummate Southern gentleman, one never to lose his temper over anything.

Well, then again, there was once. The USGA, the PGA Tour, and the PGA of America generally get along rather well. But not always.

The occasion was the USGA Annual Meeting in 1983 at The Broadmoor in Colorado Springs.

Bill presided as president, and he welcomed PGA Tour commissioner Deane Beman.

Before Deane's remarks about the state of professional golf, Bill announced the decision of the Championship Committee to raise the U.S. Open purse from $375,000 in 1982 to $500,000. The commissioner was gracious in his remarks about the 33 percent increase. We then adjourned for lunch.

Bill and Deane dined together, and the commissioner expressed his view of the growth of professional golf. Bottom line, the Open's increase of $125,000 was not keeping up with that growth.

The commissioner suggested the PGA Tour might consider conducting another Tour event at the same time as the U.S. Open. Essentially, it would be a boycott of the National Championship. To Bill Campbell, the notion that Tour players might consider skipping the Open was blasphemous—unimaginable. After lunch, Bill related the substance of their conversation. The commissioner was confident that he controlled 80 percent of the Tour's players on this proposal, but he pragmatically added that he did not have the support of the "wrong" 20 percent. The commissioner knew Palmer, Nicklaus, and Watson would always play in the U.S. Open.

The whole idea did not settle well with the USGA president.

To Bill, the U.S. Open was one of the pinnacles of golf. Prize money meant less than one's place in history.

Nearly four decades have passed since that occasion. The U.S. Open purse is now more than $12 million, an increase of 2,400 percent since 1983. The commissioner was right about the growth of professional golf.

Today, Bill Campbell would still shake his head. I am confident of that. During our last visit in October 2012, I asked if golf was still that one constant. It was not. The game had changed. Thankfully, Bill hadn't.

71

The Lighter Side
of Rules Officiating

"If you can't tell a joke, be one!"
— **Bob Murphy,** the radio voice of Stanford University athletics and my friend of fifty years.

"PREVENTIVE OFFICIATING" IS THE RIGHT PHILOSOPHY. If a penalty can be avoided, stop the player.

For example, if a player were to inadvertently tee a ball ahead of the tee markers, it made no sense for a rules official to simply watch the violation take place.

If a player could be helped by the rules, assist him. Take a moment, without delaying play, to explain the rule. Then let him make his own decision—and hope it is a prudent one.

When a ball was on a cart path, I suggested the player not pick up the ball so quickly.

"You might not like where you have to drop." I explained. "Here's the spot . . . in this bush."

Sometimes, the area of "free relief" was not really "free," and it might even result in an unplayable lie. He might be better off playing the ball from the path. In the end, the player made the decision,;I didn't, but at least the player understood the rule.

Sadly, there have been times when I arrived on the scene, only to find a player already had the ball in his hand. When he understood where he had to drop, he wanted to return the ball to the path. That could be done, of course, but at the same time the player would be adding one stroke to replace it.

The reward for assistance was often a simple "thank you" and it made being a rules official worthwhile.

Sometimes, however, assistance went underappreciated.

With preventive officiating as my guiding principle, I officiated the 1995 Tournament of Champions in beautiful Sun Valley after starting ninety women and men—all champions—who had earned the right to play Elkhorn Golf Course. Each had won a title, like the Idaho State Amateur, a club championship, or an elite amateur event.

There were so many champions the course ran out of golf carts for officials. So, Genger Fahleson and I roamed the entire course on foot. Officiating is difficult *with* transportation. We did our best without.

Despite the incredible Sun Valley setting with aspens in full color, my heart was not entirely "in" this assignment. It was yet another weekend away from home. I missed my family, my dogs, and my own golf, but my disposition was about to get worse.

While strolling the back nine and seeking relief from the doldrums, I observed the downright bad play of four men a few hundred yards away.

"What could they have won?" I asked myself.

One of the guys hit a poor shot into a lateral water hazard. From afar, I watched as he casually threw the ball to the ground about twenty feet from the stream. He had not dropped in the correct place, and he had not dropped the ball in the proper manner. None of his actions were within the rules. My first thought was to overlook the violation.

"These guys are bad," I rationalized. "They won't win anything anyway."

Then, a second thought hit me. My preventive mode kicked in.

"I owe it to the field," I thought while running to them.

"Hold up!" I yelled. The sound reverberated through the Sawtooth Mountains.

"Hold up! Hold up! Hold up!" echoed everywhere.

Tourists in nearby Ketchum might have thought there was a robbery in progress.

Now, having the attention of the foursome, I had to quickly figure out what do next. When I approached them, they seemed to think it was a real holdup. Two had clubs raised. I had no pistol drawn, just the *Rules of Golf* in hand.

Now, they viewed me not as a bank robber, but as an intruder, one who had dropped in from outer space. Their mouths were open but saying nothing. I attempted to put them as ease.

"I can help you with the rules."

It was immediately apparent. My philosophy of preventive officiating was not welcomed. Were that notion put to a vote, its defeat would have been by a 4-1 total. Amazingly, nobody told me to get lost.

"Look," I offered, "there is no penalty for dropping improperly under (old) Rule 20-6."

Their looks conveyed that I needed a padded room.

Undeterred, I continued: "Now, under (old) Rule 20-2, stand erect and drop the ball at shoulder height . . . within two-club lengths of the lateral water hazard (old). Rule 26-1 applies."

I'm pretty certain no player in this group had the slightest clue what Rule 20 or Rule 26 was about. If looks could kill, I was a goner. This posse was about to take matters into their own hands, and they were not about to be my pallbearers.

The rules violator, surprisingly, was intimidated into complying. He actually came close to holding his arm at shoulder height. I was not about to challenge him. And he dropped within two club-lengths of the stream.

Next, taking a rescue club for his next stroke, he shanked a shot about five yards—back into the water! I have never seen a non-iron go sideways—before or since. Simultaneously, all four looked at me as if I were to blame.

Three thoughts crossed my mind. "Why am I here? Why do I officiate? I'd rather be home."

Because of my informal on-course rules seminar, the player already knew how to proceed from the water. Only, this time, he dropped with his arm belt-high while glaring directly at me. His look said, "Say something. I dare you!"

Now I made the most intelligent move of the day. I made a fast getaway, slinking, and hoofing it back toward the clubhouse.

I stopped at the seventeenth green, where I finally built up the courage to ask a question of a lady who was waiting to putt.

"Do you know the fellows behind you?" I asked.

"Yes," she said.

"Do you know what tournament they've won?" I continued.

"*Won?*" she exclaimed. "We're a wedding party from Chicago!"

How these groups got onto the course in the middle of a tournament, I don't know, and I didn't sense a need to find out.

I laughed myself to sleep that night. It had been quite a day and I had done my best to prevent a penalty for dropping incorrectly under Rule 20-2a. You might have thought they would have thanked me.

72

No Room for Error Here—Scoring

A PLAYER'S NUMBER-ONE RESPONSIBILITY IN ANY COMPETITION IS TO SIGN A CORRECT SCORECARD AT THE END OF THE ROUND.

Most take this responsibility very seriously. The hole-by-hole must be accurate, and the player must sign his scorecard to certify the scores. The player is not responsible for the accuracy of addition; the committee checks that.

For obvious reasons, accuracy is imperative.

The rules are clear. If a player records a hole score on the scorecard that is higher than what was actually made, the higher score counts.

Perhaps the most famous example of this rule came at the 1968 Masters. Roberto de Vicenzo made a birdie 3 on the seventy-first hole, but playing partner Tommy Aaron, who was keeping de Vicenzo's scorecard, mistakenly wrote down a 4. Roberto did not catch the error and signed for the higher number. Thus, he scored 66 instead of 65, his correct total. Sadly, he missed the opportunity to play off against Bob Goalby, who was declared the rightful winner.

The most serious mistake is signing for a score lower than what the player actually made. The penalty is golf's "death penalty"—disqualification.

For example, if a player scored 5 on a hole but posted a 4, and the error is not corrected by the marker or player, the player is disqualified once the scorecard is returned to the committee and the player has left the scoring area. There is no exception.

In today's high-tech world, it is difficult to have scoring errors in events that involve tour professionals. A walking scorer accompanies each group at the U.S. Open. Hole-by-hole scores are immediately sent electronically upon completion of each hole to Scoring Central. Public scoreboards are then updated. The public sees them, as do the players. Bottom line, it's difficult, though not impossible, to have scoring errors today.

Sadly, it still occasionally happens for any number of reasons.

The scorecards issued on the first tee remain the official documents that certify one's score.

Because of scoring importance, the scoring area is a quiet, private, and secured area. Today, it is often a secluded office in the clubhouse, but more often it is a trailer that is tucked away in a quiet place. It is a place of consummate business.

Few are allowed access to scoring. The group includes one, perhaps two, scoring officials, the players, and sometimes their caddies and the volunteer walking scorer.

Most players meticulously mull their own scores on a hole-by-hole basis. When in doubt, they ask the marker who recorded scores. Caddies and volunteer scorers are also consulted. When a player is satisfied his hole scores are 100 percent accurate, he signs the card and gives it to the scoring officials.

The first act of the official scorer is to examine the card, looking for two signatures—the marker who recorded the scores, and the player. Without both, the scorecard is unacceptable.

If the player leaves the scoring area without signing his card, he is disqualified.

As the first-tee starter, I was often kidded because I saw the players when they were happy. That was not always the case for a scoring official. He had to deal with many who'd had a bad day. He also settled rules issues. He had to be diplomatic and sometimes empathetic. Players often were not as happy as they were on the first tee.

During my time, scoring officials were USGA staff members Tom Meeks or Tony Zirpoli.

If those officials were polled, there would probably be agreement on the one person who took the accuracy of his scorecard most seriously—Gary Player.

Nobody was like Gary. He would close his eyes, then announce his scores from memory, first forward, from 1 through 18, then in reverse order, 18 back to 1. He wasn't through yet. He'd do the same with the scoring volunteer present. Finally, he'd call his caddie and they'd go through the scores again. Gary seldom left the scoring area before the next group arrived.

Perhaps the most unusual scoring experience was provided by Bob Charles. Bob wouldn't come into the scoring area because it was usually air conditioned.

* * *

By the way, Bob also challenged the size of the hole at No. 1 at Cherry Hills Country Club in the 1993 U.S. Senior Open. Upon close inspection, he announced to referee Reed Mackenzie that the hole was too small. Fortunately, Reed was quick thinking. He folded the "Notice to Competitors" in half, making it 4-1/4 inches in width—the exact diameter of the hole. Like Cinderella's slipper, the folded sheet was a perfect fit and Reed instructed Bob to play on.

Back in the scoring area, Zirpoli dealt with a range of dispositions and attitudes. Most were gentlemanly, but occasionally he dodged scoring pencils tossed in his direction by those who had tough days. Most of those did not like the USGA's set-up of the course for the day.

Jack Nicklaus once gave Tony a heads-up before David Graham arrived in the scoring trailer. Jack had just witnessed David's five-putt from fifteen feet. Jack was correct about Graham's disposition. Tony listened to David's colorful commentary while Jack blushed.

I observed an interesting discourse between Larry Ziegler and Tony.

Larry had just bogeyed the eighteenth hole at Riviera Country Club in the 1998 U.S. Senior Open, which apparently put him in an unpleasant mood. Underscoring his unhappiness, Larry took his scorecard and put a 1 in front of the bogey 5 on the finishing hole, thereby making his score a 15. Tony attempted to reason with Larry, begging him to erase the 1 so that the scorecard reflected his true scores.

That seemed to elevate Larry's temperature even more, and to prove his point, he put another 1 in front of a second score, taking a 4 and making it a 14.

USGA president Buzz Taylor was summoned, and he, too, could not convince

Larry to correct the scores. As I observed their conversation from a distance, there was a moment when it seemed Buzz's status as an ex-Marine might be useful.

The Senior Open Rules Committee did not find humor in Larry's actions, and it disqualified him for returning an incorrect scorecard. While Larry was clearing his locker before the final round, legendary sports writer Jim Murray spotted Larry and asked where he was going.

"Home to Bay Hill," Larry quipped. "And to think, I passed up a good NASCAR race at Pocono for putting myself through this!"

Yes, there were more smiles on the first tee, but the scoring officials definitely got the better quotes.

73

This Good Deed Paid
High Dividends — to the Game

W E'VE ALL BEEN ASKED FOR A FAVOR. For people in the game, that favor involves playing golf some place. This request of me was a tough ticket.

I've lived on the Monterey Peninsula a long time, having been ordered here by the U.S. Army in 1967. There will be little weeping for us. Those orders were a blessing. We stayed.

Everyone knows we have wonderful courses here. Often, when my phone rings or an e-mail arrives, it is a friend seeking assistance in playing golf somewhere.

"Can you get me on Pebble Beach?" Or substitute *Spyglass* or *Cypress Point*, and I've heard that ten thousand times.

One of my mentors was Frank Hannigan, who, early in my years with the national governing body, got a request for assistance in playing golf. Faster than his Yankees could start a double play, Frank tossed the ball to me, a USGA rookie.

"I don't do golf," Frank said.

Well, he may have been my mentor, but I never really got his message about not "doing golf." When possible, and often luckily, we helped friends. There was never a quid pro quo. Isn't that what golfers do for friends?

One day in 1986, my phone rang. It was a young golf professional in Montana, Kevin Prentice.

Kevin had competed in the Northern California Golf Association Junior at Lake Merced Golf Club, where I'd been in charge of the event in the 1970s. Kevin was only one of the many fine young men I was fortunate to meet.

217

Kevin wanted to help two friends—Paul Caruso Jr. and Sr., from Helena, Montana. They had never played a very special course. This was a difficult request, one usually impossible. A round of gold at Cypress Point Club, in California.

"Can you help?" Kevin asked.

* * *

The gods of golf somehow aligned on our side. The Carusos had a day to remember, owing to a kind member who sponsored the father and son.

The next week, Paul Jr. called to thank me. We had yet to meet.

"What can I do for you?" he asked.

The 1986 U.S. Open was rapidly approaching at Shinnecock Hills. This Open would be the first U.S. Open for which the USGA staff would take complete responsibility—a Hannigan creation. My job for the past four years had centered on acting as player liaison—a concierge for the players. At Shinnecock Hills, we needed volunteers in the locker room and it would be all hands on deck.

"How would you like to shine shoes?" I asked my new phone pal. I was serious. There was considerable motivation. If Paul didn't say "Yes," then I might be doing it.

To my surprise, Paul accepted the invitation. He planned to drive from Helena to Southampton, New York—a little more than twenty-three hundred miles—then rent a room and pay for meals, all "for the good of the game."

For a week, the successful banker shined shoes for Nicklaus, Watson, Norman, Trevino, Floyd, and other greats of golf, as well as the wannabes, newcomers like Lehman, Azinger, and Daly, who were playing in their first U.S. Open.

A short time after we packed up and left Shinnecock Hills, I turned the tables and called Paul, wanting to help him.

"How'd you like shining shoes?" I expected the worst.

The answer surprised me. He thoroughly enjoyed it.

"What can I do now?" Paul asked

Paul Caruso proved to be a rare person for sure. Given his interest, we invited him to serve as a volunteer on the USGA's Regional Affairs Committee. His dedication caught the eye of C. Grant Spaeth, soon to be president of the association, and past president Bill Campbell. Paul was later asked to serve on the USGA Executive Committee, the first person from Montana to do so.

He ascended through the chairs, quietly rising to vice president. He attended every meeting at his own expense, and he became an expert in the rules, serving as chairman of the Rules of Golf Committee. Along the way, we teamed to bring the U.S. Junior Girls' and the U.S. Amateur Public Links Championships to Montana, another state first. Paul was cut from the same mold as Spaeth and Campbell, two of the game's best volunteers.

Paul Jr. came to golf honestly, and his dedication to the game was ingrained. His father had learned golf as a boy in western Montana. He later introduced his son to golf with sage words. "It's a game of great fairness," his dad said. They were members at Green Meadow Country Club for more than fifty years.

Paul Sr. passed away in 2015 at age eighty-nine. He was a wonderful family man, one of faith, founder of a bank, and a man of great integrity. His handicap hovered around 10, the same as his son.

Between the father, his son, and yours truly, we played golf for some two hundred years, yet owned no club titles or holes-in-one. We shared close friendships and a love of the game.

In Paul Jr., the apple did not fall far from its roots. It shined—even better than all those shoes he polished at Shinnecock Hills.

74

Frosh Hazing

I AWAITED THE NEXT GROUP WITH MORE ANTICIPATION THAN MOST. With respect to players, it was because of the official who would accompany them.

The referee was Lyn Nelson, my friend of more than thirty years. She had a distinguished career in golf—as an amateur golfer, general manager at several golf clubs, and, then, CEO of the Northern California Golf Association. She was even my boss once when I caddied for her in the California Women's Amateur.

This was Lyn's first rules assignment at the Open. I knew the excitement she felt in having this privilege.

She arrived for her 8:50 A.M. starting time on the heels of the 8:39 group. Her smile said volumes.

So did her attire. She was starched from head to foot. The shine on her golf shoes would have passed the inspection of my army drill sergeant.

"I was so proud to be wearing a sweater with that USGA emblem," she said.

She had all the tools required for the round—the *Rules of Golf*, their decisions, a hole-location sheet, a pairing sheet, and the "Notice to Competitors. "

Lyn more than passed inspection. She was perfect.

Well, there was one thing that caught my attention, and I decided to have some fun.

Lyn had the earpiece to her walkie talkie radio in her left ear.

"There's always one person who doesn't get the word," I said.

The lady turned red with embarrassment.

"What's wrong?" she asked timidly.

"In your rookie year, the earpiece should be in your right ear."

Lyn ripped it out of her left ear and moved it to her right ear. It took less time than it does for Brandt Snedeker to putt.

It took a moment for my attempt at humor to work. When Jason Gore, Arjun Atwal, and Jim Herman arrived to meet their referee, they wondered why we were laughing.

75

Out with an Old Tradition
and in with a New

O NE OF THE NICE TRADITIONS AT THE U.S. OPEN WAS THE TOAST TO THE CHAMPION. After the awards ceremony, the champion was hustled to a party of club volunteers and USGA folks, who were first to hear from the new national champion. Champagne was passed all around, and the player had a chance to thank the club and all the volunteers who help handle the millions of small details that come with the conduct of a major championship.

It was not only a memorable occasion, it often was an emotional one as the champion began to realize what was probably a childhood dream. From the Toast to the Champion, the player began a series of interviews and media obligations, and most often it was well after dark before the player finally left the club.

In 2010 at Pebble Beach, the tradition changed. There was no appearance from Graeme McDowell because media obligations took precedence.

While some at the Beach and Tennis Club might have been disappointed by the change, I wasn't. The occasion became one I'll never forget.

* * *

With a hug and a kiss from a lady friend with insider news, I learned the future of the USGA. It was then and there that I learned my friend, Mike Davis, would be named the association's next executive director. The surprise made it a special week, which also proved to be my last starting assignment, even more memorable.

Another friend, David Fay, had held that post for twenty-one years. David's tenure was second only to Joe Dey, who led the USGA for thirty-four years before becoming the PGA Tour's first commissioner. I did not know David's future plans, but after the success of the U.S. Open at two true public courses, Bethpage Black and Torrey Pines, both engineered by David, it was an auspicious time for him to spend more time watching his beloved Yankees, playing golf, reading more books, and enjoying ice cream.

I was a strong supporter of David in 1989, when he took the assignment at a most challenging time. He faced a lawsuit by Ping over its grooves, then came the issue of metal drivers having an overly generous spring effect in the faces of the clubs.

How strong a supporter of David was I? A past president, who shall also remain nameless, actually credited me with influencing David's selection. To this day, I don't believe him, but I truly thought the job required one with a strong golf-oriented background and not someone from outside the game of golf. It was rumored the selection committee was looking outside the USGA.

In my opinion, the same could be said after David retired. Mike Davis had a strong golf background, and he knew of my unending support. I encouraged him, privately, on many occasions. Still, he seemed reluctant and quite content in overseeing the "goose laying golden eggs"—the U.S. Open. I was ecstatic on hearing the news.

The world did not know until the following February. First, David announced his retirement in December 2010. Then the USGA Executive Committee confirmed Mike's selection.

I missed the old tradition, but a hug and kiss was a nice way to bring in a new one.

76

The U.S. Open's
Most Dreaded Word — Playoff

How long should a playoff be to determine the U.S. Open champion? It's not a stretch to say the USGA was debating this question the day I joined the association, and it was still at it when I left the organization more than thirty years later.

I believe our Open playoff should be eighteen holes and nothing less, but mine is not a popular opinion.

In 2018, the playoff format was changed to an aggregate score over two holes. The claim is made that this was determined by the public, players, and the media. Trust me. The vote was skewed by the latter.

Through the first 118 U.S. Opens, there were thirty-four playoffs.

The first was over eighteen holes in 1901, when Scotsman Willie Anderson prevailed over fellow countryman Alex Smith. Thirty-two other eighteen-hole playoffs were required, but interestingly, the USGA scheduled a 36-hole playoff in 1931, and Billy Burke and George Von Elm remained tied after an additional 36 holes. They must have been having a great time because they played yet another 36 before Burke won the 144-hole Open marathon.

In the 1950s, "sudden death" was adopted if players were still tied after the 18-hole playoff, but extra holes were not required for the next thirty-plus years.

Finally, in 1990, sudden-death was required after Hale Irwin and Mike Donald tied in their fifth round at Medinah. This was the first of three playoffs that ended in ties after eighteen holes. I found myself as first-tee starter in all three—1990 with

Irwin and Donald; in 1994 between Ernie Els, Loren Roberts ,and Colin Montgome-rie at Oakmont; and in 2008, the last overtime Open competition (as of 2018) be-tween Tiger Woods and Rocco Mediate.

I always thought the eighteen-hole playoff was sacred to the USGA. While the three other majors succumbed to pressure, mostly from TV and other media, I hon-esty felt the title of being the United States Open champion, the pinnacle in all of golf, was so important that the playoff format would never change. I was again wrong.

In discussions over the years, I quietly expressed an alternative to any movement to shorten the Open playoff format.

I even thought it was possible to start the Open on Wednesday. The U.S. Open is different from weekly Tour events in that it has no pro-am. Players would have at least two practice rounds, though many would have had more over the previous weekend or earlier. In the event of a tie, an eighteen-hole playoff could be accom-modated on Sunday, Father's Day. On that rare occasion of a tie on Saturday, televi-sion would have a sporting spectacle with few equals on Sunday. Fathers around the country would lie happily on their couches, glued to the TV while being served re-freshments all day.

The Wednesday start would also provide a buffer in the event of a "washout" or weather delays during Rounds 1-4. Again, TV viewers would be riveted on Sunday.

The suggestion may have died for a lack of a second.

Some who were opposed said TV ratings would suffer. My retort was simple: *au contraire*. Saturday sporting events don't seem to have a problem drawing viewers for the Kentucky Derby, the NCAA's "March Madness" semifinals, the women's finals at Wimbledon, and NCAA football every weekend in September, October, and No-vember. Conduct it properly and they'll watch.

Think of the history that went "poof" when the organization chartered to pre-serve golf history decided on a four-hole playoff. 1913, Francis Ouimet vs. England's Vardon and Ray; 1962, Palmer and Nicklaus; 2008, Tiger and Rocco.

It was a privilege to have been a part of some of golf's most memorable playoffs six times as the first-tee starter. Who knows where they'll start now?

77

Rudy's Chair

A NEW TRADITION WAS INITIATED AT CONGRESSIONAL COUNTRY CLUB IN BETHESDA, MARYLAND, IN 1997. It was known only to a few. That's the way we wanted it. The tradition became our little secret.

Dr. Tom Loss was then a practicing dentist in Seattle. His expertise with the rules had few equals, so he was a long-time volunteer at dozens of USGA championships.

At Congressional, he approached me with a special request. "Can you find a place where my dad can watch, somewhere near the first tee?" he asked.

Tom's father, Rudy, was an octogenarian, unable to walk the hills at Congressional.

It seemed reasonable enough for me. I didn't ask the committee for a ruling.

"We can do that," I said.

We could always find a quiet spot where Rudy could watch, bothering no one. A chair would be placed in front of the grandstand, where he would bother no one.

Before placing the chair, Tom, in a reversal of roles, wanted to have a "heart-to-heart" talk with his dad. Tom established some rules for Rudy. The directives had nothing to do with the *Rules of Golf.*

Son told Dad he could not talk to the players. There could be no exception. Tom knew this would be a challenge for Dad. Rudy was an affable gent from Sheridan, Wyoming, where he'd never met a stranger.

The second rule was even tougher. Rudy was ordered not to smoke. Dad finally agreed to both.

It was easy to place Rudy in front of the grandstand on the player's left. He was out of the view of TV cameras and the players. Nobody would know he was there.

Rudy took his chair at the start of play on Friday. He sat quietly, bothering no one. One rules official spotted Rudy and said he looked like "some actor."

"Yeah," the referee said, "He looks like George Burns sitting over there."

Another referee had a more interesting description. He said Rudy had a profile like the Chief on the Indian head nickel. We laughed over the description. Rudy had a stoic appearance in his front-row seat.

Before his rules assignment that day, Tom felt the need to check on his dad. He showed up at the first tee, unannounced, and his immediate reaction was the same as if he'd seen a player hit a putt at a ball that was still moving.

Tom was shocked. Rudy was having an animated discussion with David Duval. That was a clear violation of Tom's Rule No. 1—no chatting with the players. Tom sprinted across the tee to the scene.

"Dad, you're not supposed to be talking to the players!" he said.

"But, Tom, we weren't talking golf," Rudy sheepishly defended. "We were talking about fishing."

For that answer, he gave Rudy a mulligan.

Our trial experiment with Rudy was successful at Congressional. After Sunday's final round, I told Tom, "As long I'm here on the first tee, there will always be room for Rudy's chair."

The Olympic Club was next. True to my word, Rudy had a chair waiting, inconspicuously placed, bothering no one.

Again, we covered Tom's rules—no speaking or smoking. This time we added a Local Rule: "Rudy, if you need a cigarette," we told him, "'you are on the clock." He was going to be timed, just like slow golfers.

"You get five minutes to be away. Period. Then it's back to your chair." He agreed.

We did not know our Local Rule on smoking would encounter a snag.

Early in 1998, before the U.S. Open arrived, county supervisors had passed a no-smoking rule. The law was being enforced at Olympic, too.

When cigar-smoking Miguel Angel Jimenez was told about the no-smoking rule at Player Registration, he smiled and said, "Well, I guess I go home!"

Somehow, the ban was postponed for a week, so Miguel and Rudy were again happy.

Every hour, Rudy would be missing from his chair. We always knew where he was, though. Smoke billowed from behind the grandstand, giving away his location. However, he never violated the pace-of-smoking rule. The good dad got back to his chair in time.

* * *

There were no other serious issues. Rudy lived within our rules.

Next was Pinehurst in 1999. This time, the chair was there, in front of the huge grandstand, but Rudy wasn't. He was ill, then passed away in December of that year, just two months after Payne Stewart, who died tragically in October. It's a solid wager they talk a lot—mostly about fishing.

Rudy's chair sat empty for several years. Tom and I looked at it, knowing its history and symbolic importance.

There were several years when Rudy's chair was more prominently placed. That was for visits from Byron Nelson. Players took a moment to show respect for the 1939 U.S. Open champion.

In 2010 at Pebble Beach, Rudy's chair was again empty. Then I learned that Dick Falgey, a long-time friend of golf in Monterey, was struggling with health issues. Dick knew Rudy, so it seemed appropriate that he spend some time in Rudy's chair.

After he left the tournament on Sunday, we had another special guest, Lance Barrow of CBS Sports. Lance was a pal of Rudy. He paused to pay his respect and to relax for a moment before accompanying Tom Loss as a special rules observer.

2010 was my final year on the first tee, but still it brings a smile to remember the nice people who enjoyed the tradition of Rudy's chair.

78

Starter's Time

IN THE EARLY YEARS, I GOT A PERIODIC BREAK ON THE FIRST TEE. It was called a starter's time, which was a gap in the pairings. It gave the starter a chance to catch up if play had fallen behind for any reason, such as searches for lost balls.

One such break was memorable. It came at a propitious time in my first year as starter, and to my surprise, I encountered Jack Nicklaus in the restroom. He had completed the front nine holes and was headed to the tenth tee.

There was a television in the small locker room at Shinnecock Hills, and we could hear the announcer, Jack Whitaker, say, "John Mahaffey's hit. Larry Nelson's hit. We don't know where Jack Nicklaus is."

I knew where he was—washing hands, next to me.

Off he raced to the tenth tee, organizing himself along the way.

A moment later, I watched the TV and saw Jack push his tee shot badly to the right into a densely overgrown area of bushes and trees. After a five-minute search, the ball was never found. I didn't know the outcome, having returned to the first tee to continue starting groups.

After the round, Nicklaus was asked in the media center if he could remember the last time he lost a ball.

"Twenty-five years ago," he replied, though after some further research, the correct answer was two years earlier, in the British Amateur.

I'll give Jack a break on the accuracy of his response. He needed one. So did the starter.

79

Golf Is a Passport to Friendship

A MAN CALLED ME BY NAME FROM OUTSIDE THE ROPES AT MEDINAH, OUTSIDE CHICAGO, IN 1990.

"Mr. Read, Mr. Read," he started in a brogue that was unmistaken. "I want to meet the starter of the U.S. Open."

After introducing Curtis Strange, the champion from the two previous U.S. Opens, I turned to meet Hugh Ferguson.

"Mr. Read," he said. "I'm the starter at Royal Dornoch, and I'd like to meet a fellow starter."

After meeting, we exchanged addresses and for several years we corresponded. Five years later, we trudged through flurries to play at Dornoch on a cold, blustery December day.

Hugh did not want to play golf that day. He preferred a warm beverage. It was that nasty, but I'd driven from Macrihanish Golf Course, seven hours to the south. He finally acquiesced and we played fast enough that his thirst was soon satisfied. The only other golfer we saw was a gent in a kilt and one of those Scottish caps with two brims. We didn't know if he was coming or going. Given the weather, my bet was he was headed to the clubhouse.

Hugh was a wonderful guy. He became the starter at Dornoch after retiring from the British Navy. His starter's shed reminded me of a telephone booth. Rumor was that he sometimes slept in those cramped quarters.

After his retirement from the club, we met again, in 2000 at Skibo Castle nearby. This time, there was no golf, but only the renewing of our friendship.

Hugh passed away in 2010 of Alzheimer's at age eighty-eight. He lived the words of Sir Michael Bonallack at the 250th anniversary of the Royal & Ancient Golf Club, when he said, "Golf is your passport to friendship."

So did I. I'm blessed that my passport had an abundance of pages.

That statement about golf being a passport to friendship has resonated with me to this day. It describes my life. We can go back to my introduction near the front of this book, in which I write about how a guy (me) without privilege, who once got kidnapped, and who mowed his neighbor's yard, ended up on the first tee at the U.S. Open—for more than twenty years! That just boggles the mind. This has been my passport to a life full of friendships.